DATE DUE

Literature and Life series

(Formerly Modern Literature and World Dramatists)

General Editor: Philip Winsor

Selected list of titles:

SAMUEL BECKETT, *Ronald Hayman*

OLIVER GOLDSMITH AND RICHARD SHERIDAN, *Marlies K. Danziger*

CHRISTOPHER MARLOWE, *Gerald Pinciss*

SEAN O'CASEY, *Doris daRin*

JOHN OSBORNE, *Ronald Hayman*

SHAKESPEARE'S COMEDIES, *Jack A. Vaughn*

SHAKESPEARE'S HISTORIES, *George J. Becker*

SHAKESPEARE'S TRAGEDIES, *Phyllis Rackin*

BERNARD SHAW, *Pat M. Carr*

TOM STOPPARD, *Felicia Hardison Londré*

WILLIAM BUTLER YEATS, *Anthony Bradley*

Complete list of titles in the series on request.

Shakespeare's

COMEDIES

JACK A. VAUGHN

WITH HALFTONE ILLUSTRATIONS

FREDERICK UNGAR PUBLISHING CO.

NEW YORK

To my mother, Carolyn

Copyright © 1980 by Frederick Ungar
Publishing Co., Inc.
Printed in the United States of America
Designed by Edith Fowler

Library of Congress Cataloging in Publication Data

Vaughn, Jack A   1935–
  Shakespeare's comedies.

  (World dramatists)
  Bibliography: p.
  Includes index.
  1. Shakespeare, William, 1564–1616—Comedies.
I. Title.
PR2981.V3 1980   822.3'3   79–48080
ISBN 0-8044-2938-3 cloth
ISBN 0-8044-6947-4 paper

Second Printing, 1982

032587

CONTENTS

Chronology   1

Chronology	1
Comedy in Shakespeare's Time	5
The Comedies	12
The Comedy of Errors	12
The Taming of the Shrew	22
The Two Gentlemen of Verona	34
Love's Labor's Lost	45
A Midsummer Night's Dream	61
The Merchant of Venice	77
The Merry Wives of Windsor	93
Much Ado about Nothing	102
As You Like It	116
Twelfth Night; or, What You Will	130
Troilus and Cressida	143
All's Well That Ends Well	153
Measure for Measure	161
Pericles, Prince of Tyre	174
Cymbeline	185
The Winter's Tale	201
The Tempest	214
Notes	231
Bibliography	237
Index	241

CHRONOLOGY

1564   Shakespeare is born at Stratford-upon-Avon. He was christened on April 26, but his exact date of birth is unknown. It is customary to celebrate his birthday on April 23.

1582   A license is issued on November 27 for the marriage of Shakespeare to Anne Hathaway.

1583   Shakespeare's daughter Susanna is christened on May 26. (Susanna died in 1649.)

1585   Shakespeare's twin son and daughter, Hamnet and Judith, are christened on February 2. (Hamnet died in 1596, Judith in 1662).

1592   Shakespeare is by this date an established actor in London and has had at least one play produced: *Henry VI*. *The Comedy of Errors* is probably written in this year.

1593   *The Taming of the Shrew* is probably written in this year.

1594   Shakespeare is by this date a cosharer in the Lord Chamberlain's Men, together with Richard Burbage and Will Kempe. *Love's Labor's Lost* and *The Two Gentlemen of Verona* are probably written at this time.

1595 Probable date of composition of *A Midsummer Night's Dream*.

1596 Shakespeare's son Hamnet is buried in Stratford on August 11. *The Merchant of Venice* is written around this time.

1598 Shakespeare's skill as a dramatist is praised in Francis Mere's *Palladis Tamia*. The following comedies are mentioned: *The Two Gentlemen of Verona, The Comedy of Errors, Love's Labor's Lost, Love's Labor's Won, A Midsummer Night's Dream,* and *The Merchant of Venice. Love's Labor's Won* has never been identified; one theory identifies it as *Much Ado about Nothing. Much Ado about Nothing* is probably written at this time. *Love's Labor's Lost* is first printed in quarto.

1599 The Globe Theatre is built in London's Bankside district, with Shakespeare owning a one-tenth share. *As You Like It* and possibly *The Merry Wives of Windsor* are written at this time.

1600 *Twelfth Night* is probably written in this year. *A Midsummer Night's Dream, The Merchant of Venice,* and *Much Ado about Nothing* are first printed in quarto.

1601 Shakespeare's father, John, is buried in Stratford on September 8. *Troilus and Cressida* is probably written at this time.

1602 Probable date of composition of *All's Well That Ends Well. The Merry Wives of Windsor* is first printed in a "bad" quarto.

1603 Death of Queen Elizabeth on March 24. With the accession of James I, Shakespeare's company, the Lord Chamberlain's Men, becomes the King's Men, under a Patent Royal. London theaters are closed, due to a severe outbreak of plague.

1604   The public theaters reopen in April. *Measure for Measure* is probably written at this time.

1607   Shakespeare's daughter Susanna marries John Hall in Stratford on June 5.

1608   Shakespeare's granddaughter Elizabeth is christened on February 21; Shakespeare's mother is buried on September 9. Shakespeare's company leases the Blackfriars theater, with Shakespeare owning a one-seventh share. *Pericles* is probably written in this year.

1609   Probable date of composition of *Cymbeline*. *Troilus and Cressida* is first printed in quarto. *Pericles* is first printed in a "bad" quarto.

1610   *The Winter's Tale* is probably written at this time.

1611   *The Tempest* is written in this year or late in 1610; it is first performed at court on November 1.

1612   By this date, Shakespeare has returned to Stratford in retirement.

1613   The Globe Theatre burns to the ground on June 29, during a performance of Shakespeare's *Henry VIII*.

1616   Shakespeare's younger daughter, Judith, marries Thomas Queeny in Stratford on February 10. Shakespeare dies at Stratford on April 23.

1623   The first collection of Shakespeare's plays, known as the First Folio, is printed. In it appear ten comedies never before printed: *The Comedy of Errors, The Two Gentlemen of Verona, The Taming of the Shrew, As You Like It, Twelfth Night, All's Well That Ends Well, Measure for Measure, Cymbeline, The Winter's Tale, The Tempest. Pericles* is the single Shakespeare play not included in the First Folio.

COMEDY
IN SHAKESPEARE'S TIME

When young Will Shakespeare came up to London, some time between 1586 and 1590, to try his hand at writing for the stage, he found a populace already appreciative of theatrical entertainment. At a typical afternoon's performance in one of London's public theaters, one could encounter a broad cross section of the city's population. It would have been possible not only to rub elbows with the gentry but also to exchange gossip with the artisans and merchants.

Such diversity in social and economic representation was also a diversity in education and taste. It was for this reason, at least in part, that Shakespeare and his contemporaries cast their dramatic works in forms wonderfully rich and varied, freely mixing serious and comic material within a single play.

Those theatergoers on the lower end of the economic scale took their places as standees in the "pit," the ground level before the stage, and savored every bit of low comedy that the day's fare had to offer. These "groundlings" were no less important to the dramatists of the day than were the gentry seated in the galleries above. Thus we find, in even the most serious Elizabethan tragedies, scenes of foolery and comic horseplay, such as the gravediggers in *Hamlet* and the Clown's scenes in *Othello*. Audiences, then as now, love to laugh.

It is not surprising, then, that an aspiring playwright might seriously apply himself to learning the craft of comedy. This Shakespeare did, with great success. In the course of his career he produced seventeen comedies that remain today masterpieces of English drama. Much of their appeal lies in their diversity, for no two Shakespeare comedies are patterned alike. This is due in part to the wealth of source material available to the dramatist and to the variety of comic traditions within which he was able to work.

In Shakespeare's time, perhaps the most workable definition of "comedy" was "whatever is not tragedy." That is, the critical rules and guidelines for the writing of tragedy were spelled out in considerable detail, so that a tragic writer had his work carefully defined for him. Comedy, on the other hand, was a dramatic form considered distinctly inferior to tragedy, and the critics did not bother much about strict definitions of "proper" comedy. Comic dramatists, therefore, enjoyed considerable freedom of invention. Nevertheless, there were a number of influences and traditions that shaped a young writer's ideas of what it meant to write "comedy."

All drama in Shakespeare's time was grounded in the classical tradition, meaning that the playwrights and dramatic theorists looked to the ancient world for their models and critical guidelines. In comedy, therefore, a dramatist necessarily familiarized himself with the two ancient Roman playwrights Plautus (ca. 254 B.C.– 184 B.C.) and Terence (ca. 190 B.C.–159 B.C.), imitating their style and even adopting their plots. This Shakespeare did at the outset of his comic career in *The*

Comedy of Errors, the most purely classical of his comedies.

In brief, the classical tradition in comedy favored farcical plots of intrigue (usually sexual intrigue) in which the characters were little more than stereotypes —the shrewish wife, the amorous young man, the clever servant, the old lecher, and so on. The best of the English comic dramatists were able to draw upon these stereotypes as points of departure for developing fairly complex and interesting characterizations. Thus, some of Shakespeare's finest comic creations derive from the character types of the ancient Latin comedies. The Falstaff of *Henry IV*, for example, descends from the type of the miles gloriosus, or braggart soldier, and several of the low-comedy characters in *Love's Labor's Lost* owe their natures to the ancient Latin types.

The classical tradition accounts also for the Elizabethans' concept of comic dialogue. Like the Latin plays, many of the English comedies are written in colloquial, snappy dialogue filled with puns, some obscenities, and many topical allusions. Puns and wordplay were, in fact, highly popular with Shakespeare's audiences, and he never let them down in this regard.

While the audiences in the public theaters might enjoy such comedies of farcical nonsense and ribald wit, there was another audience whose tastes were more refined: the courtiers who surrounded Elizabeth. It was for this select group that a quite different comic form existed in Shakespeare's time—court comedy.

The leading writer of court comedy was John Lyly, who, primarily in the 1580s, wrote comedies for the court of Elizabeth and developed an elegant style of prose later called euphuism, after his *Euphues* (1578). English court comedy differed from the comedy of the public theaters in its refinement, its elegance of expression, and its self-congratulatory emphasis upon classical learning.

Some of Shakespeare's comedies (for example, *Love's Labor's Lost*, *A Midsummer Night's Dream*, and *The Merry Wives of Windsor*) are known to have been performed at court, attesting to his skill in writing for the pleasure of a courtly audience. Although he almost never indulged in the extreme euphuistic style, Shakespeare learned much from Lyly and developed his own style of elegant expression for the dialogue of some of his comedies. This influence is seen especially in the early comedies, such as *The Two Gentlemen of Verona* and *Love's Labor's Lost*. (In the latter, Shakespeare mocks euphuism through the pretentious characters of the subplot.)

Still another major tradition that influenced Shakespeare and his contemporaries in the writing of comedy was that of the romance. Much of the Elizabethan comic plot material is derived from the medieval and Renaissance literature that extolled romantic love and idealized the relationship between the sexes. Shakespeare drew upon such story material in his last four comedies especially, but the tradition can be seen also in *The Two Gentlemen of Verona*, *A Midsummer Night's Dream*, *Troilus and Cressida*, and others.

A particularly rich source for dramatic plots of romantic intrigue was the narrative fiction of Renaissance Italy—especially the *novelle*, or collections of short stories, that so delighted English readers. Shakespeare frequently adapted these Italian tales, in both tragedy and comedy. *Othello*, for example, is based upon a tale by Giraldi Cinthio (1504–1573), and both *All's Well That Ends Well* and *Cymbeline* owe their intrigue plots to the *Decameron* of Boccaccio (1313–1375).

The Italianate plot material of romantic intrigue was nicely complemented in Elizabethan comedy by the literary tradition of courtly love, a most important convention in almost every one of Shakespeare's comedies. Derived from Renaissance lyric poetry (especially the love sonnet, as written by literary gentlemen in honor of their ladyloves), the courtly-love tradition is at the heart of almost every depiction of romantic love in Shakespeare.

According to the convention, a lover experiences great emotional disturbances, involving even physical pain. His symptoms include pallor, trembling, loss of appetite, sleeplessness, sighing, and weeping. His distress is often described in terms associated with burning: flames, furnaces, sparks, and fires. In Shakespeare's early comedies, courtly lovers abound. By the time of *As You Like It* and *Twelfth Night*, however, we find Shakespeare gently spoofing the artificiality of the tradition through characters like Orlando and the duke Orsino. This shift in attitude toward conventional romance accords with Shakespeare's tendency, around the turn of the century, to turn away from romantic comedy and experiment with other forms—especially realistic comedy and tragicomedy.

In 1598 Shakespeare's friendly rival Ben Jonson earned considerable success with his comedy *Every Man in His Humour*, which introduced a new type of realistic, contemporary satire to London audiences. The type became known as the "comedy of humours." It concentrated on strong, clearly identifiable character types, assigning to each figure some dominant trait or disposition (a "humour") that determined his behavior in any dramatic situation.

The Elizabethan comedy of humours, which greatly influenced Shakespeare and his contemporaries around 1600, was almost always satiric in intent, subjecting to extreme ridicule contemporary follies and foibles. Plot situations were usually based upon intrigues and tricks played by clever schemers upon unsuspecting gulls. Characters were usually assigned names that described their obsessive dispositions. Shakespeare's major venture in the genre was *Twelfth Night*, but his general trend toward realistic comedy is evident also in *Much Ado about Nothing*, *The Merry Wives of Windsor*, *Troilus and Cressida*, *All's Well That Ends Well*, and *Measure for Measure*.

In roughly the first decade of the seventeenth century, yet another comic tradition evolved; that of tragicomic romance. Tragicomedy, developed principally by John Fletcher (1579–1625) and Francis Beaumont (1584–1616), was designed to appeal to the Jacobean audience's fondness for emotion and sentiment, contrived suspense, sensationalism, and visual spectacle. Writers of tragicomedy, Shakespeare included, attempted to frame plots with tragic implications, keeping their characters on the brink of disaster, only to effect their happy rescue in the play's final moments. The tragicomic style evidently appealed to Shakespeare's artistic sense, for he not only ventured upon it but brought it to near perfection in his last plays, particularly in *The Winter's Tale* and *The Tempest*.

Comedy in Shakespeare's time was as rich and varied as any body of literature ever produced in English. Inclusive of such diverse traditions as classicism, medieval romance, courtly love, Italianate intrigue, realistic *humours* comedy, and tragicomedy, it provided a wealth of happy matter for its audiences. And nowhere is this wealth more evident than in the plays of William Shakespeare. In his seventeen comedies Shakespeare proved himself a master of dramatic structure, language, and characterization. He brought English drama to a level of excellence seldom since equaled.

Shakespeare was a genius in the art of plot construction. In utilizing source material, he drew upon well-known tales of intrigue and romance and transformed them from simple narrative entertainments into dramatic actions of considerable complexity. He out-shown all his contemporaries in unifying two, three, and sometimes even four separate story lines into a single dramatic plot.

In versification, too, Shakespeare led the field. His comedies, rich in poetic imagery, utilize diverse styles of language: rhymed verse, blank verse, elegant prose, and the colloquial English of his fellow Londoners. No other dramatist of his day had so great a facility with language.

It is perhaps, however, in the art of characterization that Shakespeare most clearly surpassed his fellow dramatists. His characters remain among the finest in the world's dramatic literature. The figures of his comedies—Petruchio, Puck, Shylock, Beatrice and Benedick, Rosalind, Imogen, Prospero—are eternal, as alive today as they were when they first issued from the pen of their creator, four hundred years ago.

Shakespeare's comedies are among the world's greatest literary works; to know them is to know something of joy.

THE COMEDIES

The Comedy of Errors

Comic plots of mistaken identity are as old as the drama itself. They delighted the ancient Greeks and Romans, as well as the Elizabethans, no less than they captivate today's viewers of television sitcoms. It is not surprising, then, that Shakespeare, in writing one of his earliest comedies (perhaps his very first), turned to the best-known example of the type—the *Menaechmi* of Plautus.

The Comedy of Errors follows the plot of the *Menaechmi* fairly closely, but Shakespeare's additions and alterations add to the fun of the original, while at the same time endowing Plautus' thin farce with some resonance and feeling. In this early and somewhat trivial comedy, Shakespeare gave a clear indication of his ability to make an audience laugh.

The *Menaechmi* is a simple comedy in which two identical twins are repeatedly mistaken for each other. Shakespeare turned the Menaechmus twins into Antipholus of Syracuse and Antipholus of Ephesus, separated as infants and now arrived at the same city, Ephesus. Shakespeare added the characters of Aegeon, father to the twins, and Aemilia, an abbess who turns out to be their mother. Luciana, Adriana's sister, is also Shakespeare's original.

Most importantly, however, Shakespeare added a second pair of twins, doubling the servant Messenio from Plautus into the two Dromios, servants to the two Antipholuses. The idea for twin Dromios was probably suggested to Shakespeare by another Plautine comedy, the *Amphitruo*, which is also the source for the scene in *The Comedy of Errors* (III, i) in which Antipholus and Dromio of Ephesus are denied admittance to their own home while Antipholus' wife entertains the boys from Syracuse. With a double set of twins, Shakespeare quadrupled the fun and was able to introduce considerable complexity into this most meticulously plotted of his comedies.

The Comedy of Errors is a fine example of farce, the type of comedy in which characterization is subordinate to the intricacies and movement of the plot. Its characters do not cause the action to happen; they are, rather, the victims of the central situation—of the gimmick. The presence of two sets of twins in the same city is a precondition of the action, and what we witness is the result of that state of affairs. Moreover, there is not one character who knows the situation or can explain the confusion. This sets *The Comedy of Errors* apart from Shakespeare's other comedies of mistaken identity.

Shakespeare was to use mistaken identity extensively in his later comedies (for example, *A Midsummer Night's Dream*, *As You Like It*, and *Twelfth Night*), but in every case there is either an element of deliberate deception at work or at least an awareness by one or more characters of the true situation. *The Comedy of Errors* is utterly free of deception; there is no schemer, or "practicer," who causes the confusion (save Shakespeare himself). And no character is aware of the truth. Antipholus of Syracuse, who has come to Ephesus expressly to search for his identical twin, never suspects that his strange encounters result from mistaken identity. Such absurdities are allowable in farce.

The plot of our farce does not, in the usual sense, advance. There are no developments, no shifts in course, no new complications—only variations on a theme. Once the given situation—two sets of identical twins in the same town—is established, Shakespeare takes us through no fewer than seventeen episodes in which "errors" are committed. His skill in orchestrating these variations is dazzling. Exits and entrances are plotted with meticulous care to keep each twin separated from his fellow. Every possible combination of characters is assembled and exploited in a rapid succession of encounters. Shakespeare is a juggler, keeping all his characters (and his audience) in midair, allowing none to fall to the dull earth of realism until it is time to end the performance.

This zaniest of all Shakespeare's plots begins, however, on a curiously somber note. The farce of the two sets of twins is framed by the touching drama of old Aegeon, father to the Antipholus twins, who opens the comedy with a pathetic tale of past woe—the shipwreck in which he, his wife, their twin sons, and the twin companions were separated long ago. Such tales of shipwrecks, separated families, and eventual reunions were well known and popular with Shakespeare's audience. They derived from the ancient tale of Apollonius of Tyre, upon which source Shakespeare was later to draw for *Pericles, Twelfth Night, Cymbeline,* and *The Winter's Tale.*

Aegeon and his misfortunes are not heard of again until the final scene (V, i), at which point we find one of the most artificial climaxes in any of Shakespeare's comedies. When the Abbess comes forth from the priory with Antipholus and Dromio of Syracuse, the simultaneous presence of both sets of twins on stage makes obvious the source of all the "errors." Then, to add to the surprise, the Abbess, upon seeing Aegeon, reveals that she is his long-lost wife Aemilia and, therefore, the mother of the Antipholus twins.

This denouement is pure deus ex machina; there is not one line earlier in the play to prepare us for this turn of events. Surprising endings are certainly appropriate in farce, but Shakespeare's later practice was always to foreshadow such miraculous occurrences and coincidences.

The framing action of Aegeon's little domestic drama, with its emphasis upon the restoration of familial ties, gives *The Comedy of Errors* a resonance and depth of feeling that transcends simple farce. It is perhaps a mark of Shakespeare's comic genius that he was henceforth always to introduce a note of seriousness into even the most frivolous of comic stories. As Hardin Craig noted in his edition of the comedy:

> Shakespeare loved to play with edged tools. Somebody's life, or somebody's happiness must be at stake even in his comedies. . . . After the introduction of the good Aegeon with his moving appeal to the magistrate to spare his life . . . we never get him out of our minds, and, in the midst of the fun and confusion, we continue to wonder if he will be saved.[1]

Shakespeare's improvements upon his source were not limited to plotting and structure. In the creation of characterization he also transcended his model. Plautus' comedy is pure farce, created solely for the purpose of evoking laughter. Thus, its characters are one-dimensional stereotypes—the shrewish wife, the parasite, the courtesan, and so on—who merely perform the actions required by the plot. Shakespeare changed that.

Antipholus of Syracuse, the central character of the

comedy, wins our sympathy from the first, as he explains his reason for coming to Ephesus:

> I to the world am like a drop of water
> That in the ocean seeks another drop,
> Who, falling there to find his fellow forth,
> Unseen, inquisitive, confounds himself:
> So I, to find a mother and a brother,
> In quest of them, unhappy, lose myself.[2]
>
> (I, ii)

Once the "errors" commence, he becomes confused and disoriented at his apparent transformation into a being other than what he knows himself to be:

> Am I in earth, in heaven, or in hell?
> Sleeping or waking? mad or well-advised?
> Known unto these [Adriana and Luciana], and
> to myself disguised.
>
> (II, ii)

When in the same scene he is chided by Adriana (who believes him to be her husband) for keeping from home and neglecting his conjugal duties, he can respond only with wide-eyed wonder:

> How can she thus then call us by our names?
> Unless it be by inspiration.
> . . . .
> What, was I married to her in my dream?
> Or sleep I now and think I hear all this?
> What error drives our eyes and ears amiss?

Although we, the audience, can laugh heartily at Antipholus from our superior vantage point, knowing the true source of the "errors," we are nevertheless touched by Shakespeare's sympathetic portrayal of a young man whose identity is in question and whose sense of self is threatened.

Antipholus of Syracuse achieves added dimension in his encounter with Luciana (III, ii), who thinks him to be her brother-in-law. She chides him for treating her sister so badly, neglecting his home, and consorting with another woman. Her lecture, rather than prompting him to get to the bottom of the confusion, sparks a romantic flame and he declares his love for her:

> O train me not, sweet mermaid, with thy note,
> To drown me in thy sister's flood of tears:
> Sing, siren, for thyself and I will dote:
> Spread o'er the silver waves thy golden hairs,
> And as a bed I'll take them and there lie,
> And in that glorious supposition think
> He gains by death that hath such means to die:
> Let Love, being light, be drowned if she sink!

This brief scene (seventy lines), written in quatrains and couplets, is the single instance of romantic love in the comedy, but it is enough to add a new dimension to the bemused Antipholus—one totally absent from Plautus.

Shakespeare made other significant alterations in his source through his characterizations of the Wife (who has no proper name in Plautus) and the mistress of Menaechmus I, whom Plautus called Erotium. In the Latin original, the more important of the two roles is that of Erotium, whose relationship with Menaechmus is exclusively sexual. Shakespeare reduced the role to a minimum (a mere thirty-five lines) and made her a "hostess" with whom Antipholus of Ephesus goes to dine after being denied entrance to his own home. It is noteworthy that she is the only character in the comedy, aside from the merchants, without a proper name. She is referred to in the list of dramatis personae and in her speech headings as "Courtezan," but that term is never spoken on the stage. To the audience, she is simply a pretty hostess. Typically, Shakespeare tempered the coarse sexuality of his source.

More significant is what Shakespeare did with the Wife, creating the very individual character of Adriana. Plautus' character plays a very small role and is presented, typical of Roman comedy, as a scolding shrew—one whom Menaechmus is all too happy to abandon at the comedy's close. Shakespeare's Adriana has sympathetic qualities and is multidimensional.

Adriana serves as an effective foil to Luciana, who advocates total submission to the dominance of the male. Adriana will have none of that and protests that the wife, too, has rights within the marriage bond (II, i). The two sisters have been likened to Kate and Bianca in *The Taming of the Shrew*, but Adriana is no mere shrew who requires taming. Her love for Antipholus is genuine, and she more than once frankly expresses her devotion to her husband as well as her dependence upon him. Thinking herself addressing her spouse, and puzzled by his strangeness, she pleads with Antipholus of Syracuse:

> How comes it now, my husband, O, how
>   comes it,
> That thou art thus estranged from thyself?
> . . . .
> Ah, do not tear away thyself from me!
> For know, my love, as easy mayst thou fall
> A drop of water in the breaking gulf
> And take unmingled thence that drop again,
> Without addition or diminishing,
> As take from me thyself and not me too.
>
> (II, ii)

Hardly the utterance of a shrew! And when her husband sends for bail money to obtain his release from the Officer, she responds without hesitation and sends the required sum. Finally, when she believes her husband to be mad and hiding in the priory (although it is actually Antipholus of Syracuse) she comes to take him home:

> I will attend my husband, be his nurse,
> Diet his sickness, for it is my office,
> And will have no attorney but myself . . .
>
> (V, i)

What shrewishness there is in Adriana's behavior is occasioned by the sincere sense of wrong that she feels at her husband's neglect of home and hearth. As she herself states, after cursing him in a moment of anger, "My heart prays for him, though my tongue do curse" (IV, ii).

In modifying his source, then, Shakespeare added to the basic farce the drama of individual characters caught up in a truly distressing misunderstanding. He established convincing relationships between his figures and created for us the sense that what happens to them matters. And this was achieved without sacrifice of the broad humor and delightful confusions that are so enjoyable to an audience.

The Comedy of Errors is great fun on the stage. It abounds with physical action, including a number of beatings, as well as considerable variety in its styles of language—prose, blank verse, couplets, quatrains, and crude doggerel. Some of its scenes are downright hilarious—for example, the pun-laden dialogue between Antipholus and Dromio of Syracuse (II, ii), which plays like vaudeville cross talk or an Abbott and Costello routine; the scene in which their Ephesus counterparts are denied access to their house (III, i); and Dromio of Syracuse's Rabelaisian account of being wooed by the corpulent kitchen wench Nell (III, ii).

The Comedy of Errors in a carnival setting at the Oregon Shakespearean Festival (Ashland) in 1976. Directed by Will Huddleston; scenic design by Richard L. Hay; costume design by Jeannie Davidson; lighting design by Thomas White.

HANK KRANZLER

Despite its rich offering of low comedy, however, the play has not had an illustrious stage history. It was infrequently performed until it gained some popularity in 1734, in an adapted version called *'Tis All a Mistake*. It continued to be played only in adapted form until 1855, when Samuel Phelps revived Shakespeare's original version at Sadler's Wells. The comedy is probably best known to twentieth-century audiences through its musical adaptation by Rodgers and Hart, *The Boys from Syracuse* (1938).

A most inventive production of *The Comedy of Errors* was staged at the Oregon Shakespeare Festival in Ashland in 1976. The setting was a carnival. The two Dromios were clowns, the Antipholuses wore wild-animal trainers' costumes, and the residents of Ephesus included harem dancers, acrobats, a gorilla, and other appropriate characters. The carnival metaphor worked quite well until the appearance of the Abbess, played as a gypsy fortune-teller. Whatever implications there may be in Shakespeare's comedy of the Abbess as a figure of Christian charity (and some critics have suggested this), they were not present in this production.

The Comedy of Errors is not a great play, when viewed in the light of Shakespeare's later comedies, but it can make a delightful evening of theater when played with energy, sharp comic timing, and style.

The Taming of the Shrew

The Taming of the Shrew, written probably in 1593 or 1594, is one of Shakespeare's best known and most frequently staged comedies. It expands upon a theme explored somewhat superficially in *The Comedy of Errors*: the appropriate roles for husband and wife within the marital relationship. In fact, it is perhaps due to this comedy's spirited and entertaining portrayal of the "battle of the sexes" that it is so popular with audiences today.

This comedy is one of Shakespeare's earliest (if not his very first) attempts at multiplotting, and his success is admirable. He drew upon at least two sources, interweaving quite disparate stories with considerable inventiveness. The principal Petruchio-Kate action is taken from an earlier comedy of undetermined authorship called *The Taming of a Shrew* (first printed in 1594), and the Bianca-Lucentio involvement derives from an English translation of an Italian comedy, George Gascoigne's *Supposes* (1566), after Ariosto's *I Suppositi* (1509). This latter source also influenced the plot of *The Comedy of Errors*.

It is the story of Petruchio, who woos, weds, and finally beds the shrewish daughter of Baptista Minola, Katharine (called Kate), that so delights modern audiences. This story follows closely the plot of the earlier *A Shrew* play, although the exact relationship between the two works has not been established. It has been maintained variously that *A Shrew* is Shakespeare's earlier play, which he reworked into *The Shrew*; that *A Shrew* was written by another dramatist; and that both plays are based upon yet a third and earlier *Shrew* play that is lost. In any case, we are indebted to *A Shrew* and Shakespeare's improvements upon it not only for the great fun of the Petruchio-Kate plot but also for the rather puzzling feature of the Christopher Sly induction.

The induction, a fairly common device in Elizabethan drama, is an opening scene that prepares the audience by stating frankly that they are about to see a dramatization. This theatrical device sets the audience at one remove from the drama by pointing out that the play to follow is just that—a play and not a real occurrence. The drama itself, then, is technically a play-within-a-play.

The induction to *The Taming of the Shrew* shows us Christopher Sly, the drunken tinker for whose benefit the play-within-a-play is performed. This framing action closely resembles its original in *A Shrew* but for one notable exception. In the source play Sly and his fellows remain on stage to the end, commenting from time to time on the action; Shakespeare abandons them after the opening scene (except for four lines at the end of I, i), and the comedy of Petruchio's conquest of Kate proceeds without further reference to the inductive framework.

We can only speculate on Shakespeare's reasons for beginning his comedy with an induction presenting characters to whom he never returned, but G. B. Harrison offers a plausible explanation in the introduction to his edition of the comedy:

> This manner of presenting a play as part of a dream or story is a useful convention, especially when the theme of the play is to be wild and fantastic, for the Induction is a bridge between the fantasy and the hearer's sense of reality. It may be that the author of *The Taming of the Shrew* was saying in effect to the hen-pecked husbands in his audience: "A drunkard's dream, my friends—but don't you wish that it was true!"[1]

The wooing of Bianca by her three suitors, which constitutes the subplot of this comedy, is an important part of the whole. Based upon disguise and intrigue, it follows its source, Gascoigne's *Supposes*, fairly closely. It is, in the words of Hardin Craig, "one of the best examples in English of the Italian comedy of intrigue."[2]

Shakespeare's audience would have understood well the convention that the younger sister (Bianca) could not marry before the older one (Kate). Thus, Kate's shrewish disposition stands as a direct obstacle to Bianca's happiness, and the suitors court in vain. Least attractive of the suitors is Gremio, an old but wealthy Paduan. His character is derived from the commedia dell'arte stock character of Pantalone, a traditional figure of foolishness. (Lucentio refers to him at one point as "old pantaloon.") Hortensio, the second suitor, is younger but no more successful.

It is Lucentio, a young scholar from Florence, who wins Bianca's heart and eventually weds her. Lucentio is the ideal lover. He exemplifies most of the traditions of courtly love, a convention in Italian and English Renaissance literature that extolled neo-Platonic idealism above physical love. True to the convention, Lucentio falls in love with Bianca at first sight:

> O, Tranio, till I found it to be true,
> I never thought it possible or likely;
> But see, while idly I stood looking on,
> I found the effect of love in idleness:
> And now in plainness do confess to thee,
> . . . .
> Tranio, I burn, I pine, I perish, Tranio,
> If I achieve not this young modest girl.
>
> (I, i)

His new-found love can be described only through elevated classical allusions:

> O yes, I saw sweet beauty in her face,
> Such as the daughter of Agenor had,
> That made great Jove to humble him to her hand,
> When with his knees he kiss'd the Cretan strand.

She represents all that is perfect and innocent:

> Tranio, I saw her coral lips to move
> And with her breath she did perfume the air:
> Sacred and sweet was all I saw in her.

Within the courtly-love tradition, the eyes were supposed to be the windows of the soul, and Lucentio speaks of "that maid/Whose sudden sight hath thrall'd my wounded eyes."

In all respects, the Lucentio-Bianca courtship is depicted as idealized romance. Shakespeare's intention in this regard becomes even more clear if one looks at his source. In *Supposes*, the Bianca character, Polynesta, is pregnant by her lover Erostrato (Lucentio here) from the outset. As in *The Comedy of Errors*, Shakespeare altered his source to mitigate coarse sexuality.

Bianca is, as a character, somewhat colorless and far less interesting than Kate. She is seen to be an obedient daughter, and she encourages Lucentio's courtship without being immodest. Dramatically, of course, she is drawn as a foil for Kate—obedience and compliancy vis-à-vis defiance and perversity. It is especially ironic, then, that by the final scene of the comedy the two sisters have changed roles. It is Bianca who refuses to come at her husband's bidding and Kate who lectures her on wifely obedience.

There is some amount of charm and wit in the subplot of *The Taming of the Shrew*, although it is peopled with conventional character types—the virtuous maiden, the clever servant, the courtly lover, the old Pantalone, and so forth. Perhaps it is only in contrast with the very vivid figures of Petruchio and Kate in the main plot that these characters pale.

The contrasts between the Petruchio-Kate plot and the Lucentio-Bianca plot are sharp. While the latter depicts idealized courtship and romance, Petruchio's "courtship" is realistic and earthy, if somewhat extravagant. The Lucentio action is a typical plot of intrigue and deception, but Petruchio's involvement with Kate is absolutely straightforward and devoid of any deception. When Petruchio first appears, he reveals his motives to Hortensio in unequivocal terms:

> Signior Hortensio, 'twixt such friends as we
> Few words suffice; and therefore, if thou know
> One rich enough to be Petruchio's wife,
> As wealth is burden of my wooing dance,
> Be she as foul as was Florentius' love,
> As old as Sibyl and as curst and shrewd
> As Socrates' Xanthippe, or a worse,
> She moves me not, or not removes, at least,
> Affection's edge in me, were she as rough

As are the swelling Adriatic seas:
I come to wive it wealthily in Padua;
If wealthily, then happily in Padua.

(I, ii)

This is no starry-eyed lover—no courtly figure who will woo in elegant verse. He is out simply to make a profitable match. Petruchio's essential role in the comedy is one of husband, not lover. And it is the conditions of marriage that are considered in the Petruchio-Kate plot, not courtship, as in the Lucentio-Bianca intrigue.

Petruchio can have no illusions about the fabled shrew Katharine, for the others are quick to tell him quite frankly what to expect. Hortensio, who would certainly wish to see Kate married off as quickly as possible so that he might succeed with Bianca, describes the shrew with brutal frankness:

> Her only fault, and that is faults enough,
> Is that she is intolerable curst
> And shrewd and froward, so beyond all
>   measure
> That, were my state far worser than it is,
> I would not wed her for a mine of gold.
> . . . .
> Her name is Katharina Minola,
> Renown'd in Padua for her scolding tongue.
>
> (I, ii)

In the same scene old Gremio learns that Petruchio will go after "Kate the curst" and can hardly believe it:

> Hortensio, have you told him all her faults?
> . . . .
> O Sir, such a life, with such a wife, were
>   strange!
> But if you have a stomach, to't i' God's name:
> You shall have me assisting you in all.
> But will you woo this wild-cat?

This "wild-cat" Kate is a fascinating figure. We are made to feel that her shrewishness is not true to her essential nature and that her eventual "taming" is simply a return to rational behavior—a rediscovery of her natural self. The alteration in her personality during the course of the play gives her considerable depth for a character of farce.

In her first appearance, we see Kate living up to her reputation for a "scolding tongue" as she abuses Gremio, Hortensio, and her sister. It is noteworthy, however, that she speaks only in response to some fairly uncomplimentary remarks made at her expense by the two suitors to Bianca. In Act II, scene i, we see her abusing her sister, whose hands she has bound. She strikes Bianca, but when Baptista breaks up the quarrel, Kate tells us what is on her mind:

> What, will you not suffer me? Nay, now I see
> She is your treasure, she must have a husband;
> I must dance bare-foot on her wedding day
> And for your love to her lead apes in hell.

She is jealous of the attentions being paid to Bianca and fearful of becoming an old maid. What we have seen of her curst behavior to this point is extreme, but it is not without motivation.

The audience is well prepared, then, for the first meeting of Petruchio and Kate; our expectations have been so aroused, in fact, that this initial encounter is one of the special moments in Shakespeare. It is often played with a long silence in which the two adversaries size each other up before the battle begins. Some directors use the moment to establish an immediate and powerful sexual attraction between the two.

Petruchio takes the offensive at once by calling her Kate. She protests that she is called Katharine, but he challenges her: "You lie, in faith; for you are call'd plain Kate,/And bonny Kate and sometimes Kate the curst" (II, i). Their "courtship" scene then takes the form of a battle of wits as the two engage in elaborate punning and abusive repartee. He resorts to outrageous sarcasm, applying to her the very terms that a serious lover might employ—"passing gentle," "pleasant, gamesome, passing courteous," and "sweet as spring-time flowers." But she will have none of it and he must close the interview by stating frankly that she will be his, willing or not:

> PETRUCHIO. Am I not wise?
> KATHARINE. Yes; keep you warm.
> PETRUCHIO. Marry, so I mean, sweet Katharine,
> in thy bed:
> And therefore, setting all this chat aside,
> Thus in plain terms: your father hath
> consented
> That you shall be my wife; your dowry
> 'greed on:
> And, will you, nill you, I will marry you.

This "wooing" scene is conventionally played with a great deal of physical and even violent action, sometimes to the point of suggesting a wrestling match. Yet there is in the text only one indication of violence between the two. Kate strikes him, and he responds: "I'll cuff you, if you strike again." It can be an effective moment, for no matter how unwilling she may be to marry him, at this point she knows that he means business.

From this scene forward, Petruchio employs a consistent strategy in his taming of the shrew. He behaves in an outrageous and irrational manner—arriving late for his own wedding dressed in bizarre attire; carrying his new bride off with the absurd accusation that her own family means to steal her away; and denying her food and sleep under the pretext of being extra solicitous of her well-being. (He himself calls it "a way to kill a wife with kindness.") What he accomplishes is to illustrate for her the harmful effects of irrational and extreme behavior—behavior of which she herself has been guilty in her shrewishness.

The turning point in their relationship comes when he has so subjugated her to his will that he can claim arbitrarily that the sun is the moon, and she will agree (IV, v). Kate learns obedience, but more importantly she learns to see herself as others have seen her. The portrait is not flattering. In a sense, Petruchio acts as a mirror for her through his own abusive behavior toward his servants, toward the Tailor, and toward the Haberdasher.

Petruchio rekindles human feeling in Kate. When he strikes his servants she protests, although she had earlier struck her own sister with less provocation. By the time her conversion is complete, she is once again a natural, feeling woman. What is more important, she is now suited to assume the role of wife, which is, in Shakespeare's understanding of nature, the ultimate destiny of woman. As Petruchio had told her in the "courtship" scene, "Women are made to bear, and so are you."[3]

Kate's final speech chastising Bianca and the Widow for their disobedience and cataloguing the duties that a wife owes her husband creates a difficult moment on the stage today. Our attitudes toward the role of women differ significantly from those in Shakespeare's time, and the speech is frequently played tongue-in-cheek or with understanding glances between Petruchio and Kate that belie her words. It is not uncommon today for this speech to elicit derisive laughter or cat-calls from the feminists in the audience when Kate claims that "Thy husband is thy lord, thy life, thy

The American Conservatory Theatre's (San Francisco) successful *Taming of the Shrew*, 1974. Petruchio (Marc Singer) "courts" Katharine (Fredi Olster). Shown also on national television, the production was directed by William Ball.

WILLIAM GANSLEN

keeper,/Thy head, thy sovereign," or that "Such duty as the subject owes the prince/Even such a woman oweth to her husband."

Nevertheless, this speech is central to the serious theme with which Shakespeare was dealing in the Petruchio-Kate plot: the need for harmony and understanding within the marital bond. Such harmony is essential if the race is to propagate and if domestic life is to prosper. In *The Taming of the Shrew* Shakespeare makes a case for the natural order of things in marriage. It is a case that he was to make repeatedly in his later comedies.

The Taming of the Shrew has long been one of Shakespeare's more popular comedies on the stage. It offers fast-moving fun, with colorful characters and snappy, realistic dialogue. The comedy's language is clear and direct; even its blank-verse passages are easy on the ears of modern listeners. It has, in fact, been called the least poetical of Shakespeare's plays.

The comedy was adapted in 1667 by the Restoration actor John Lacy as *Sauny the Scot,* a dreadful version that held the stage for decades. In 1754 David Garrick produced a fairly faithful version called *Catharine and Petruchio,* from which the induction was omitted, as is usually the case today. In 1837 Shakespeare's original version was presented by Benjamin Webster, and another successful production followed in 1856 at Sadler's Wells, produced by Samuel Phelps.

The first notable American production of *The Taming of the Shrew* was that produced by Augustin Daly in New York in 1887. With John Drew and Ada Rehan in the leading roles, it ran for 121 performances. (The induction, incidentally, was performed as written.) Also successful for years as Petruchio and Kate were E. H. Sothern and Julia Marlowe around the turn of the century.

More recently, Alfred Lunt and Lynn Fontanne had great success as Petruchio and Katharine, touring the country in a version that kept Christopher Sly onstage until the end. The comedy has gained added attention in its musical-comedy adaptation, *Kiss Me, Kate* (1948), by Cole Porter. A successful film version was made in 1967 with Richard Burton and Elizabeth Taylor in the leading roles.

An outstanding production of *The Taming of the Shrew,* by San Francisco's American Conservatory Theatre in 1974, delighted audiences not only in that city but throughout America when it was produced on national television. The production was directed by

William Ball, who chose to emphasize the play's commedia dell'arte background and transformed the work into a dazzling, knockabout farce. The scenes between Petruchio and Kate (Marc Singer and Fredi Olster) resembled a cross between a wrestling match and a gymnastics exhibition. The induction was omitted, but Ball framed the play within a commedia dell'arte troupe performance, with the actors setting the stage and inviting the audience to enjoy. And enjoy they did. It was a brilliant production of this most stageworthy Shakespeare comedy.

The Two Gentlemen of Verona

The Two Gentlemen of Verona (1594–95) is one of Shakespeare's least performed and least appreciated comedies. Although it offers a degree of charm and lighthearted fun, the play is of interest not so much for what Shakespeare achieved in it as for what he promised. In it we find an early sampling of actions, themes, and characters that were to be developed and refined in the later comedies.

The story of *The Two Gentlemen of Verona* is a typical one of Italianate love intrigues, based upon an early Spanish pastoral romance, *Diana Enamorada*, by the Portuguese writer Jorge de Montemayor (1520–1561). An earlier English play from this same source, *The History of Felix and Philiomena*, is known to have been acted at court in 1584–85 and may have influenced Shakespeare, but it is lost. In adapting the source story to the demands of the stage, Shakespeare created a comedy that conforms to the literary traditions of courtly love, honor, and male friendship.

The Two Gentlemen of Verona presents a number of problems, attributable either to carelessness on Shakespeare's part or to textual revision and tampering by other hands. There are elements of plot and character that are poorly handled within the total structure of the play. The character of Eglamour, for example, is introduced abruptly only to effect Silvia's escape. He is a stick figure from medieval knight-errantry whose sole purpose is to serve a lady in distress. Having done so, he disappears from the play.

Problematic also is Proteus's abrupt shift of affections from Julia to Silvia. Although it stems from the love-at-first-sight convention, it stretches our credulity by its suddenness and its flimsy justification—a simile or two from Proteus:

> Even as one heat another heat expels,
> Or as one nail by strength drives out another,
> So the remembrance of my former love
> Is by a newer object quite forgotten.
>
> (II, iv)

Then, as though the playwright himself were struggling with a difficult plot twist, Proteus works out, in a tortuous and sophistical soliloquy (II, vi), an elaborate justification for abandoning Julia and betraying Valentine. (His shift of affections puts us in mind of another lover: Romeo, who renounces his Rosaline at the sight of Juliet, but with far greater dramatic credibility.)

The entire business of the outlaw band, which dominates the fourth and fifth acts, is barely credible and only loosely related to the main action. The outlaws perform no necessary function in the plot, except perhaps to provide, with their "shadowy desert [and] unfrequented woods," a momentary pastoral counterpoint to our city-bred gentlemen and ladies. Moreover, it is absurd that the outlaws should, upon first seeing Valentine, appoint him as their leader solely because he is "beautified/With goodly shape and . . ./A linguist" (IV, i).

Although we should never hold Shakespeare accountable for geographical accuracy (the Bohemia of *The Winter's Tale* has a seacoast!) and might overlook Valentine's traveling from Verona to Milan by water, there are troubling confusions in place names in the Folio text. The Duke refers to his Milan at one point as Verona; Valentine tells Thurio, a Milanese courtier, "Verona shall not hold thee"; and Speed welcomes Launce to, of all places, Padua. These minor errors lend support to the theory of textual corruption—a theory that helps to explain the play's major problem, namely, Valentine's abrupt and unmotivated forgiveness of Proteus's treachery in the final scene (V, iv). It is a problem that causes some difficulty in performance, for both gentlemen are made to display complete reversals of attitude within a dozen or so lines of dialogue.

Valentine is totally unaware that his dearest friend Proteus has betrayed him to the Duke and has attempted to court his (Valentine's) beloved Silvia. In concealment, Valentine watches Proteus not only ask Silvia's favor but also lay violent hands upon her in an effort to force her to yield. Valentine steps out and confronts the would-be seducer, catching Proteus with, as it were, his breeches down:

> VALENTINE. Ruffian, let go that rude uncivil
>   touch,
>   Thou friend of an ill fashion!
> PROTEUS.   Valentine!
> VALENTINE. Thou common friend, that's
>   without faith or love,
>   For such is a friend now; treacherous man!

Valentine berates Proteus for an additional nine lines, concluding with: "The private wound is deepest: O time most accurst,/'Mongst all foes that a friend should be the worst!" Proteus's remorse and repentance are immediate:

> My shame and guilt confounds me.
> Forgive me, Valentine: If hearty sorrow
> Be a sufficient ransom for offence,
> I tender 't here; I do as truly suffer
> As e'er I did commit.

Immediate too is Valentine's forgiveness:

> Then I am paid;
> And once again I do receive thee honest.
> Who by repentance is not satisfied
> Is nor of heaven nor earth, for these are pleased.

And then, as though forgiveness were insufficient: "And, that my love may appear plain and free,/All that was mine in Silvia I give thee."

It is at that point that Julia swoons, and small wonder! The swiftness of Proteus's repentance, followed immediately by Valentine's forgiveness and offer of Silvia to Proteus, has led the New Cambridge editors to suggest textual cutting and revision of the final scene by hands other than Shakespeare's. It is a persuasive theory, but it may be, too, that we have the scene precisely as the playwright intended it, notwithstanding its abrupt reversals. For *The Two Gentlemen of Verona* is a play not only about love but also, as its title seems to suggest, about friendship.

The obligations of honor and respect attendant upon male friendship were well understood in Shakespeare's time. The tradition can be traced back to Cicero's *De Amicitia*, and many Elizabethan writers had penned poems and plays extolling the supremacy of male friendship over romantic love. John Lyly, a writer who influenced Shakespeare's early work, stated the case for friendship quite strongly in his court comedy *Endimion* (ca. 1588). Thus, Shakespeare's audience was familiar with the convention and may well have understood perfectly when Valentine makes the ultimate gesture of honor toward the repentant Proteus—surrender of his claim to Silvia in deference to his friend's interests.

It is worth nothing also that this theme—friendship in conflict with romantic love—is present in the sonnets that Shakespeare wrote at approximately this same time (1593–96). Sonnet 42 reflects upon a situation that closely resembles the Valentine-Silvia-Proteus complication. Sonnet 34 is addressed to a repentant friend and expresses Shakespeare's grief at the wrong his friend has done him; it concludes, suggestive of Valentine: "Ah! but those tears are pearl which thy love sheds,/And they are rich and ransom all ill deeds." And in Sonnet 40, the poet invites his friend, a rival in love, to "take all my loves," rather than destroy their friendship. Clearly, the issue of friendship was very much on Shakespeare's mind at the time *The Two Gentlemen of Verona* was written.

In some respects, this play might be viewed as a "love-versus-honor" comedy in this counterposing of romance and friendship. Within the English courtly-love tradition, upon which Shakespeare drew quite heavily here, romantic love is an honorable undertaking the end of which is holy matrimony. Love cannot succeed when the lover forsakes his friends and resorts to duplicity—not, at least, in comedy. In Valentine and Proteus we see exemplified honorable and dishonorable love, respectively.

Valentine, as his name suggests, is the true lover. He pursues his wooing of Silvia in the courtly manner. At the outset he scoffs at love, but at the sight of Silvia, true to the convention, he becomes love's slave:

> I have done penance for contemning Love,
> Whose high imperious thoughts have punish'd
>   me
> With bitter fasts, with penitential groans,
> With nightly tears and daily heart-sore sighs;
> For in revenge of my contempt of love,
> Love hath chased sleep from my enthralled eyes
> And made them watchers of mine own heart's
>   sorrow.

> (II, iv)

For Valentine, "Love's a mighty lord," and the young gentleman exhibits all the symptoms of the happy affliction that is courtly love.

Proteus, on the other hand, is false to both friend and lover. He lives up to his namesake, the Greek god who could change his shape at will. In the first scene of the play he claims that his love for Julia has "metamorphosed" him. When he and Valentine part, he sees it as an estrangement of honor from love:

> He after honour hunts, I after love:
> He leaves his friends to dignify them more;
> I leave myself, my friends and all, for love.

In Milan, Proteus is once again metamorphosed when he sees Valentine's ladylove, Silvia. He renounces his love for Julia and attempts to woo his best friend's girl. The cad proves himself without honor and utterly self-seeking in his rationalization of this dishonorable conduct toward both Julia and Valentine:

> To leave my Julia, shall I be forsworn;
> To love fair Silvia, shall I be forsworn;
> To wrong my friend, I shall be much forsworn.
> . . . .
> Julia I lose and Valentine I lose:
> If I keep them, I needs must lose myself;

> If I lose them, thus find I by their loss
> For Valentine myself, for Julia Silvia.
> I to myself am dearer than a friend.
>
> (II, vi)

Thus, forsaking honor and friendship, he breaks his sacred vow of love to Julia and betrays his sworn friend to the Duke, bringing about Valentine's banishment from Milan. Proteus disrupts the moral equilibrium of this comedy's world. Balance is to be restored only when he finally repents his treachery and is forgiven by Valentine. The Christian ideals of repentance and forgiveness bring love and honor back into accord.

Shakespeare's chief success in *The Two Gentlemen of Verona* was in creating characters who transcend the stereotypes of the courtly-love genre. Some of the figures in this comedy point to characters that were to appear in the later comedies.

Most important in this respect is the unhappy Julia. The plot device of the unfortunate maiden donning boy's clothing and following her beloved was a conventional one in Renaissance fiction. Shakespeare was to employ it again with Viola (*Twelfth Night*), Rosalind (*As You Like It*), and Imogen (*Cymbeline*). Julia is their prototype, although she is a charming character in her own right. As the unfortunate victim of Proteus's treachery, she is a woman of some feeling —affecting in her sorrow. But she is also a creature of spirit and fun. She banters with her maid Lucetta (I, ii) as they discuss her suitors (a type of scene to be developed more fully for Portia in *The Merchant of Venice*) and feigns indifference to Proteus. She tears up his love letter, but once Lucetta exits, she shows us her true feelings in a charming soliloquy:

> O hateful hands, to tear such loving words!
> Injurious wasps, to feed on such sweet honey
> And kill the bees that yield it with your stings!

I'll kiss each several paper for amends.
Look, here is writ 'kind Julia.' Unkind Julia!
As in revenge of thy ingratitude,
I throw thy name against the bruising stones,
Trampling contemptuously on thy disdain.
And here is writ 'love-wounded Proteus.'
Poor wounded name! my bosom as a bed
Shall lodge thee till thy wound be throughly
  heal'd;
And thus I search it with a sovereign kiss.

Like Viola, Julia is sent to woo her own rival in her beloved's behalf. And like the best of Shakespeare's wronged ladies, she is stoic in her distress and ever constant to the cad who has betrayed her. Even when Proteus sends her to Silvia with the very ring with which she (Julia) swore her love to him, she quickly regains her composure and maintains her disguise:

PROTEUS. Go presently and take this ring with
    thee,
  Deliver it to Madam Silvia:
  She loved me well deliver'd it to me.
JULIA. It seems you loved not her, to leave her
    token.
  She is dead, belike?
PROTEUS.   Not so; I think she lives.
JULIA. Alas!
PROTEUS.   Why dost thou cry 'alas'?
JULIA.   I cannot choose
  But pity her.
PROTEUS. Wherefore shouldst thou pity her?
JULIA. Because methinks that she loved you as
    well
  As you do love your lady Silvia:
  She dreams on him that has forgot her love;
  You dote on her that cares not for your love.
  'Tis pity love should be so contrary;
  And thinking on it makes me cry 'alas!'
                                    (IV, iv)

Comic servants are a vital ingredient in the recipe of Shakespearean comedy, and *The Two Gentlemen of Verona* provides us with a double dose: Speed (Valentine's man) and Launce (Proteus's). Speed is the witty, garrulous punster, in the tradition of the Dromios in *The Comedy of Errors* and of Grumio and Biondello in *The Taming of the Shrew*. In Shakespeare's later works, the type was sometimes drawn as a fool or jester, such as Feste (*Twelfth Night*) and Touchstone (*As You Like It*).

Speed's scenes, although bright and swift-moving, present some of the more difficult language of the play, for his speeches are full of wordplay—puns, conceits, and quibbling (a special kind of elaborate punning of which Elizabethan audiences were especially fond). Speed provides a realistic counterpoint to the highly artificial and conventional ladies and gentlemen of the love plot. He scoffs at the courtly-love convention and twits his love-smitten master for falling under Silvia's spell:

> VALENTINE. Why, how know you that I am in love?
> SPEED. Marry, by these special marks: first, you have learned, like Sir Proteus, to wreathe your arms, like a malecontent; to relish a love-song, like a robin-red-breast; to walk alone, like one that had the pestilence; to sigh, like a schoolboy that had lost his A B C; to weep, like a young wench that had buried her grandam; to fast, like one that takes diet; to watch, like one that fears robbing; to speak puling, like a beggar at Hallowmas. . . . And now you are metamorphosed with a mistress, that, when I look on you, I can hardly think you my master.
> (II, i)

Although Speed provides much of the brightness in what is a fairly somber love story, for modern audiences the comic highlight is Launce, an original in Shakespeare's gallery. While some of Speed's wit is difficult, Launce's simple humor is immediate and hilarious. He is the prototype of the "natural" or dim-witted clown who was to appear again and again in Shakespeare's comedies—Costard in *Love's Labor's Lost*, Bottom in *A Midsummer Night's Dream*, Dogberry in *Much Ado about Nothing*, the nameless Clown of *The Winter's Tale*, and others. Launce is a naive and earthy buffoon who, with his dog Crab, provides the low comic relief in this play. Crab emerges almost as a character in his own right:

> I think Crab my dog be the sourest-natured dog that lives: my mother weeping, my father wailing, my sister crying, our maid howling, our cat wringing her hands, and all our house in a great perplexity, yet did not this cruel-hearted cur shed one tear: he is a stone, a very pebblestone, and has no more pity in him than a dog.
>
> (II, iii)

The obdurate Crab, we later learn, disgraces Launce at the Duke's table by snatching a chicken leg from Silvia's plate, upsetting the company with his odor, and—most unforgiveably—answering the call of nature, to Launce's mortification:

> Nay, I remember the trick you served me when I took my leave of Madam Silvia: did not I bid thee still mark me and do as I do? when didst thou see me heave up my leg and make water against a gentlewoman's farthingale? didst thou ever see me do such a trick?
>
> (IV, iv)

Although Launce and Crab furnish the fun of *The Two Gentlemen of Verona*, the clown has no part to play in the movement of the plot. He exists, in a sense, outside the action. It is possible that Shakespeare created the role simply as a vehicle for Will Kempe, his leading comedian. Kempe, a skilled comic, undoubtedly made Launce seem indispensable. As H. B. Charlton has stated: "He has no real right within the play, except that gentlemen must have servants, and Elizabethan audiences must have clowns."[1] And we, too, are the richer for Launce and Crab.

For whatever reasons, *The Two Gentlemen of Verona* has never been popular on the professional stage. It is rarely produced except by companies dedicated to the production of the entire Shakespeare canon. Its absence from the theater is unwarranted, for when it is produced it proves to be an enjoyable and charming comedy, notwithstanding its unlikely plot reversals. The play is best known to contemporary audiences in its very popular rock-musical version, which first appeared in 1971 as a production of the New York Shakespeare Festival. Most of the musical's dialogue is taken directly from Shakespeare, who probably would have approved of the musical treatment. The rock *Two Gentlemen of Verona* highlights perfectly the charm, exuberance, and lighthearted fun inherent in Shakespeare's play.

Love's Labor's Lost

"... formless and fantastic in plot."
"... deficient in plot and in characterization."
"The whole play is a very silly one."
"If we were to part with any of the author's comedies, it should be this one."

These comments are typical of those with which
critics until recently have attempted to dismiss *Love's
Labor's Lost* as a minor comedy of questionable worth
—a flawed, early work. Then, in 1936, the English stage
director Tyrone Guthrie mounted the play at London's Old Vic in a dazzling production that delighted
the critics. It proved finally that in *Love's Labor's Lost*
Shakespeare did indeed know what he was doing. Since
that time this play, neglected by producers for two
centuries, has come into its own and received serious
attention as a Shakespeare comedy unlike any other,
and a viable work for the stage.

What Guthrie discovered in his production was
that *Love's Labor's Lost* is, to quote the clownish
Costard, "a great feast of languages"—a comedy of
conversation. It is also a sort of linguistic ballet. Its
formal patterns of poetry determine its shape and

movement, much as a musical score determines a dance. Guthrie virtually choreographed the work, emphasizing the connection between the visual and the aural.

The music and movement of language is the richness of *Love's Labor's Lost*. In modern criticism of the comedy, musical references abound. John Dover Wilson claimed that the "spirit of the whole is far more like that of a Mozart opera . . . than anything we are accustomed to in modern drama."[1] G. B. Harrison went so far as to call *Love's Labor's Lost* a "musical comedy, a revue, a trifle for the amusement of a select audience at a Christmas house party."[2]

Harrison's reference to Christmas is based on the knowledge that Shakespeare wrote this comedy for performance at court (possibly as early as 1593) and that it was played before Elizabeth and her courtiers at Christmas in 1597. It is an appropriate work for such an occasion, for its concern is with games and pastimes, and it culminates in the delightful pageant of the Nine Worthies (V, ii)—a play-within-a-play that is also a royal-entertainment-within-a-royal-entertainment.

Since he intended it for a courtly audience, Shakespeare filled *Love's Labor's Lost* with topical references, and much of the courtiers' enjoyment must have derived from their recognition of its allusions to contemporary figures. Thus, a great deal of critical ink has been poured over the text in an attempt to learn who the comedy's characters are meant to represent—especially the ridiculous figures of the subplot. Is Holofernes a satiric attack on the Italian scholar John Florio, or on Thomas Jenkins, Shakespeare's Stratford schoolmaster? Is Moth really Thomas Nashe, Armado a spoof of John Lyly, and Nathaniel a swipe at Robert Greene? The questions can never be satisfactorily answered, nor need they be for our enjoyment. Shakespeare's story stands on its own merits.

Love's Labor's Lost is one of the few Shakespeare

plays for which no literary source has been found, although there may have been one. The story derives, rather, from historical occurrences, freely adapted by the dramatist. There was, for example, a king of Navarre who in 1578 and 1586 received embassies from France. Similarly, the names of Shakespeare's courtiers—Berowne, Dumain, and Longaville—are those of men actually associated with the court of Navarre. However, Shakespeare's organization of this historical material into a dramatic plot is, evidently, his original work.

The plot of *Love's Labor's Lost* is simple and predictable, offering few surprises. Vows of celibacy in dramatic comedy are made to be broken. Berowne, the comedy's chief courtier, tells us that "these are barren tasks, too hard to keep,/Not to see ladies, study, fast, not sleep" (I, i). When he reminds the King that the Princess of France is due to arrive, we know for certain that courtship is in the offing. And when she arrives with three companions, we know that the courtship will be fourfold.

This courtship quartet is played in a purely conventional manner. Although each of the four gentlemen swears love, gives gifts, writes sonnets, and rhapsodizes on the perfections of his lady, there is something slightly impersonal about it all. The ladies, for example, permit the wooings only in a spirit of jest. Although they express admiration for their suitors, at no time are we led to believe that they love in like degree. As the Princess tells the suitors, after hearing of her father's death:

> We have received your letters full of love;
> Your favours, the ambassadors of love;
> And, in our maiden council, rated them
> At courtship, pleasant jest and courtesy
> As bombast and as lining to the time:

> But more devout than this in our respects
> Have we not been; and therefore met your
>   loves
> In their own fashion, like a merriment.
>
> (V, ii)

The lovers, moreover, although paired off, appear as a group throughout the play. We never see a single pair alone, and the wooing is always marked by witty repartee. Berowne sets the tone for the others in his talk of love. His concern is principally with how *he* feels—the heightening of his powers and perceptions. (see IV, iii) At no time is he concerned with love as an experience between two people. C. L. Barber has said that *Love's Labor's Lost* illustrates the "folly of acting love and talking love, without being in love."[3]

We are not unduly distressed, therefore, when all this love play comes to naught. Although Mercade's announcement of the French king's death (V, ii) is a jolt (and, incidentally, a stunning dramatic effect in the playing), it seems right that the Princess turns her attention to her grief and rejects Navarre's suit:

> KING. Now, at the latest minute of the hour,
>   Grant us your loves.
> PRINCESS.   A time, methinks, too short
> To make a world-without-end bargain in.

Each of the ladies instructs her suitor to wait one year before resuming his courtship. But Berowne and the King are to bear an additional burden. The Princess tells the King to "go with speed/To some forlorn and naked hermitage" and live an "austere insociable life" until the year is past. Rosaline's sentence on Berowne is even more harsh. As a corrective to his "gibing spirit," which is "replete with mocks . . . and wounding flouts":

> You shall this twelvemonth term from day to
>   day
> Visit the speechless sick and still converse
> With groaning wretches; and your task shall
>   be,
> With all the fierce endeavour of your wit
> To enforce the pained impotent to smile.

Berowne consents to the task and observes:

> Our wooing doth not end like an old play;
> Jack hath not Jill: these ladies' courtesy
> Might well have made our sport a comedy.

Thus is love's labor lost. And it is fitting, in both thematic and dramatic terms, that it should be so. The gentlemen's original oath—a stoical rejection of the pleasures of life—is, in Shakespeare's scheme of things, unnatural. It represents a denial of life and it must be corrected. Moreover, their forsaking of Love, within the courtly-love tradition, constitutes heresy, for which penance must be served before the prize is won.

However appealing the courtship games of the main plot of *Love's Labor's Lost*, the characters who play the games are but lightly sketched. With the exception of Berowne, there is little distinction among the four gentlemen of Navarre. The King, according to Granville-Barker, "remains a bundle of phrases," and Dumain and Longaville "have about the substance of echoes."[4] The ladies fare somewhat better. While Katharine and Maria are virtually indistinguishable, we have some sense of individuality in Rosaline and in the Princess—the latter because of her role as spokesperson for the group.

Berowne and Rosaline emerge as the most interesting of the courtly figures. They exemplify a type of love relationship that Shakespeare was later to develop more fully with Beatrice and Benedick in *Much Ado about Nothing*. At their initial encounter (II, i), we see how the love game will be played:

> BEROWNE. Did not I dance with you in Brabant once?
> ROSALINE. Did not I dance with you in Brabant once?
> BEROWNE. I know you did.
> ROSALINE. How needless was it then to ask the question!
> BEROWNE. You must not be so quick.
> ROSALINE. 'Tis 'long of you that spur me with such questions.
> BEROWNE. Your wit's too hot, it speeds too fast, 'twill tire.
> ROSALINE. Not till it leave the rider in the mire.
> BEROWNE. What time o' day?
> ROSALINE. The hour that fools should ask.
> BEROWNE. Now fair befall your mask!
> ROSALINE. Fair fall the face it covers!
> BEROWNE. And send you many lovers!
> ROSALINE. Amen, so you be none.

This same sort of witty banter marks most of their encounters in the play. When Berowne falls hopelessly in love with her, against his will and contrary to his oath, we know it is not merely the physical that attracts him but also the intellectual. All four couples engage in some degree of verbal sparring, but in courtly conversation Berowne and Rosaline excel.

By far the stronger characterizations in *Love's Labor's Lost* are those of the comedy's subplot: Armado, Moth, Holofernes, Nathaniel, Costard, Dull, and Jaquenetta. Whatever their reference to contemporary figures, these characters are delightful in their own right. They are Shakespeare's originals, even though they derive from stock character types dating back to ancient Latin comedy.

These same type characters were common, too, in the Italian commedia dell'arte, upon which Shakespeare obviously drew in creating his band of Navarre commoners. Armado's bravado recalls the braggart captain of the commedia; Holofernes descends from the Doctor; Costard is typical of the *zanni*; Nathaniel plays the parasite; and so on. That Shakespeare had in mind the traditional character types is obvious in the Folio text, where their speech headings are frequently their generic names: Braggart, Pedant, Clown, Boy. (Shortly before the pageant of the Nine Worthies is performed in V, ii, Berowne refers to the performers as "the pedant, the braggart, the hedgepriest, the fool and the boy.")

Shakespeare wrote *Love's Labor's Lost* at a time when the English language was rapidly evolving and expanding—virtually exploding—with new forms, new words, and a changing syntax. This comedy shows, more than any of his other plays, the exuberance of a young poet testing his resources, pushing his material to the limit, stretching wit and wordplay to extremes. The comedy is conscious of its language. Time after time the courtly figures congratulate themselves on a set of wit well played or a barbed pun well aimed. Of course, Shakespeare did not develop this style of dialogue singlehandedly. Other courtly poets were similarly occupied, notably John Lyly, whose elegant prose style, later called euphuism (after his *Euphues*), influenced *Love's Labor's Lost*.

The play's dialogue is highly poetic and richly varied. It contains more rhymed lines than any other Shakespeare play, including couplets, quatrains, sextets, octaves, and even whole sonnets. Its blank-verse passages, although few, are expressive, and its prose passages range from the convoluted euphuism of Armado to the direct, homespun utterances of Costard and Dull. There are throughout the play many correspondences to passages from the sonnets that Shakespeare was composing at the same time.

Various kinds of linguistic affectation are satirized in the characters themselves, especially Armado, Holofernes, and Costard. Armado's love affair with his vocabulary is made clear to us even before his first entrance. The King describes him as

> A man in all the world's new fashion planted,
> That hath a mint of phrases in his brain;
> One who the music of his own vain tongue
> Doth ravish like enchanting harmony.
>
> (I, i)

He then reads Armado's letter to him, the salutation of which is "Great deputy, the welkin's vicegerent and sole dominator of Navarre, my soul's earth's god, and body's fostering patron."

When Armado then appears before us (I, ii), we see ridiculed all the preciosity of courtly utterance. In declaring his love for the country wench Jaquenetta, he expresses his passion with neatly balanced phrases:

> I do affect the very ground, which is base, where her shoe, which is baser, guided by her foot, which is basest, doth tread. I shall be forsworn, which is a great argument of falsehood, if I love. And how can that be true love which is falsely attempted? Love is a familiar; Love is a devil: there is no evil angel but Love. Yet was Samson so tempted, and he had an excellent strength; yet was Solomon so seduced, and he had a very good wit. Cupid's butt-shaft is too hard for Hercules' club; and therefore too much odds for a Spaniard's rapier.

When the Princess first hears Armado she observes that he "speaks not like a man of God his making," and Holofernes says of him:

> He is too picked, too spruce, too affected, too
> odd, as it were, too peregrinate, as I may call
> it. . . . He draweth out the thread of his
> verbosity finer than the staple of his argument.
> (V, i)

Holofernes should be the last to talk! Himself
ridiculously affected, he is the epitome of pedantry,
with his boorish Latin and his strings of synonyms.
Referring to a deer that the Princess has slain in the
hunt, he declares:

> The deer was, as you know, sanguis, in blood;
> ripe as the pomewater, who now hangeth like
> a jewel in the ear of caelo, the sky, the welkin,
> the heaven; and anon falleth like a crab on the
> face of terra, the soil, the land, the earth.
> (IV, ii)

Proud of his ability to "something affect the letter"
(compose alliteratively), he speaks an "extemporal
epitaph" on the death of the deer, which begins: "The
preyful princess pierced and prick'd a pretty pleasing
pricket." It grows worse as it goes along.

This same slain deer gives Holofernes the opportunity to display his contempt for the untutored when
the simple Dull mistakes Holofernes' Latin *haud credo*
for "awd (old) grey doe" and protests that it was no
doe but a pricket (young buck). Holofernes responds:

> Most barbarous intimation! yet a kind of in-
> sinuation, as it were, in via, in way, of explica-
> tion; facere, as it were, replication, or rather,
> ostentare, to show, as it were, his inclination,
> after his undressed, unpolished, uneducated,
> unpruned, untrained, or rather, unlettered, or
> ratherest, unconfirmed fashion, to insert again
> my haud credo for a deer.

Costard and Dull, simple country folk, give us the opposite end of the scale of linguistic abuse— simplicity to the point of stupidity. Dull can make no sense of anything that Holofernes and the fawning Nathaniel say. With elaborate condescension, the latter diagnoses Dull's deficiency:

> Sir, he hath never fed of the dainties that are bred in a book; he hath not eat paper, as it were; he hath not drunk ink: his intellect is not replenished; he is only an animal, only sensible in the duller parts.
>
> (IV, ii)

On the few occasions when Dull enters the conversation, his malapropisms ("reprehend" for "represent," "farborough" for "tharborough," "collusion" for "allusion," and so on) suggest a model for Dogberry in *Much Ado about Nothing*.

Costard, on the other hand, uses his simplicity to serve his own turn. Beneath his pretensions of ignorance we see a mind quick to turn language to comic advantage. When accused by the King of enjoying the pleasures of the flesh with Jaquenetta (I, i), he invokes a string of synonyms to evade the charge:

> KING. It was proclaimed a year's imprisonment, to be taken with a wench.
> COSTARD. I was taken with none, sir: I was taken with a damsel.
> KING. Well, it was proclaimed "damsel."
> COSTARD. This was no damsel neither, sir; she was a virgin.
> KING. It is so varied too; for it was proclaimed "virgin."
> COSTARD. If it were, I deny her virginity: I was taken with a maid.
> KING. This maid will not serve your turn, sir.
> COSTARD. This maid will serve my turn, sir.

If the commoners show us language debased by ignorance, pretension, and pedantry, the ladies and gentlemen of the court provide conversations of elegance and true wit. The four ladies, left to themselves, have little to do but engage in punning and wordplay:

> KATHARINE.   Had she been light, like you,
>   Of such a merry, nimble, stirring spirit,
>   She might ha' been a grandam ere she died:
>   And so may you; for a light heart lives long.
> ROSALINE. What's your dark meaning, mouse,
>   of this light word?
> KATHARINE. A light condition in a beauty dark.
> ROSALINE. We need more light to find your
>   meaning out.
> KATHARINE. You'll mar the light by taking it
>   in snuff;
>   Therefore I'll darkly end the argument.
> ROSALINE. Look, what you do, you do it still i'
>   the dark.
> KATHARINE. So do not you, for you are a light
>   wench.
> ROSALINE. Indeed I weigh not you, and there-
>   fore light.
> KATHARINE. You weigh me not? O, that's you
>   care not for me.
> ROSALINE. Great reason; for "past cure is still
>   past care."

And the Princess closes the exchange with:

> Well bandied both; a set of wit well play'd.
>   (V, ii)

The "set of wit" wrings every possible meaning out of "light" (merry, casual, fair-complexioned, illumination, wanton, lightweight) and "dark" (obscure, brunette, without light, secret), as well as incidental puns on "snuff" and "weigh."

The gentlemen too have their way with words—especially Berowne, who is given to euphuistic phrase-balancing and alliteration, as well as to rhyme and the irresistible pun:

> Why, all delights are vain; but that most vain,
> Which with pain purchased doth inherit pain:
> As, painfully to pore upon a book
>   To seek the light of truth; while truth the
>   while
> Doth falsely blind the eyesight of his look:
>   Light seeking light doth light of light
>   beguile:
> So, ere you find where light in darkness lies,
> Your light grows dark by losing of your eyes.
>
> (I, i)

Formal balance of words and phrases, such as that in the passage above, characterizes much of the dialogue of *Love's Labor's Lost*. But this same kind of structural balancing can be seen in the comedy as a whole, especially through alternation and parallelism in episodes, characters, and language styles. The play divides neatly into two halves of nearly equal length. The first half (through the end of Act IV) culminates in the gentlemen's vow to abandon study and celibacy, and in their "resolve to woo these girls of France." The second half shows the wooing game. Throughout the comedy, verse scenes of courtly wit alternate with the earthy prose of the commoners.

The court of Navarre is represented by four young gentlemen; the French embassy, by four young ladies. They are neatly paired off in their affections—the King with the Princess, Berowne with Rosaline, Longaville with Maria, Dumain with Katharine. The elderly Boyet serves as a pivotal character around whom these four couples revolve.

The Muscovite masquerade of Act V, scene ii, illustrates Shakespeare's skill in suggesting choreography for these nine characters through their dialogue. In making sport with their admirers, the four ladies exchange the favors sent to them and don masks. They are flanked at one side of the stage, and the masquers enter at the other. Boyet serves as go-between, passing back and forth with their communications:

> ROSALINE. What would these strangers? know
> their minds, Boyet.
> . . . .
> BOYET. What would you with the princess?
> BEROWNE. Nothing but peace and gentle
> visitation.
> ROSALINE. What would they, say they?
> BOYET. Nothing but peace and gentle visitation.
> ROSALINE. Why, that they have; and bid them
> so be gone.
> BOYET. She says, you have it, and you may be
> gone.
> KING. Say to her, we have measured many
> miles
> To tread a measure with her on this grass.
> BOYET. They say, that they have measured
> many a mile
> To tread a measure with you on this grass.

As the exchange continues, Boyet himself comes near to measuring a mile as he treads from group to group.

When the music begins, the couples pair off (though each man has the wrong lady) and each couple, in turn, comes forward to play a brief scene in which the lady bests the gentleman in a set of wit. After the final set, Boyet steps forth with his choruslike commentary:

> The tongues of mocking wenches are as keen
> As is the razor's edge invisible,
> Cutting a smaller hair than may be seen,
> Above the sense of sense; so sensible

> Seemeth their conference; their conceits have
>   wings
> Fleeter than arrows, bullets, wind, thought,
>   swifter things.

The dialogue suggests the movement. Boyet is in the center as the couples circle slowly around him to the music, each couple arriving down center for their exchange. Shakespeare has suggested here a dance pattern, and this is but one example.

The commoners are balanced, too, each with a contrasting character. The courtly, somber Armado stands in relief against the diminutive and nimble Moth, a spirited page who is never still. Costard's witty wisecracks contrast the utterances of "most dull, honest Dull." And Holofernes' pedantic and pretentious pronouncements are all the more ludicrous for the enthusiasm with which the parasitic Nathaniel snaps them up, fearful of losing a syllable of the master's discourse. Only the country wench Jaquenetta seems to lack a foil. But then, she is wooed by both Armado and Costard—a fulcrum supporting two ludicrous extremes of love.

Other parallels and contrasts abound. The oaths of celibacy of Act I become oaths of love in Act IV. The serious study to which the gentlemen aspire in the first half is mocked by the pointless pedantry of Holofernes in the second. The neo-Platonic love that exalts the four gentlemen is contrasted to the carnal desires of Costard and Armado for Jaquenetta (who, we are told, is two months pregnant at the end). Throughout the comedy, one finds formal patterns, implied movement, and a kind of compositional balance that can be fully realized only in the theater.

Love's Labor's Lost was evidently popular with its original courtly audiences, for it was revived in 1605

A fanciful nineteenth-century setting for *Love's Labor's Lost* at Stratford, Ontario, in 1974. Pictured are (rear, left to right) the King of Navarre, the Princess of France, Maria, and Katherine; (front) Berowne and Rosaline. Director, Michael Bawtree; designer, Sam Kirkpatrick.

ROBERT C. RAGSDALE, F.R.P.S.

for the pleasure of King James I and Queen Anne. It may have been played again around 1630 (It was reprinted in 1631) before it slipped into its two-hundred-year retirement from the stage. Charles James Mathews brought it back to the theater in 1839 at Covent Garden, with Mme. Vestris playing Rosaline, and a notable production by Samuel Phelps appeared at Sadler's Wells in 1857.

American productions of the comedy date from Augustin Daly's 1874 version in New York. In 1891, the younger John Drew and Ada Rehan appeared as the King and the Princess in another New York production.

But the production that assured *Love's Labor's Lost* a place on the modern stage was the Guthrie version previously mentioned, in 1936. The noted Shakespeare scholar John Dover Wilson viewed that production with great enthusiasm and singled out the principal feature of *Love's Labor's Lost* that makes it valid for audiences today:

> Its structure may be mechanical, its plot feeble, its "apprehension of life" shallow—as the critics allege—but it *goes*, goes with a swing and an impetus which, when seen on the stage, are irresistible. For sheer gaiety none of Shakespeare's other comedies can beat it.[5]

A Midsummer Night's Dream

One could hardly imagine a more unlikely combination of comic plot materials than that of classical Greek mythology, English fairy lore, Italianate love intrigue, and Elizabethan amateur theatricals. Yet that is precisely the mélange that Shakespeare concocted in *A Midsummer Night's Dream*, the play that most critics agree is his first wholly satisfactory comedy.

The virtue of the piece lies partly in Shakespeare's successful blending of disparate plot elements into a unified whole, and partly in the poetic advances that he made here over his four previous comedies. In *A Midsummer Night's Dream* Shakespeare wove the threads of four distinct actions into a tapestry of magical enchantments and courtly festivity, creating a complexity in multiplotting far greater than that of any of his earlier comedies. And in its verse and imagery he achieved a successful union of poetry and drama—a considerable advancement over, for example, the mannered formalism and self-conscious badinage of *Love's Labor's Lost*.

The plot material for *A Midsummer Night's Dream*

is largely Shakespeare's invention, although he borrowed minor features of his tale from a variety of sources. From the medieval romance of *Huon of Bordeaux*, for example, derives the idea for Oberon, King of the Fairies. Chaucer's *Knight's Tale* provided the marriage of Theseus and Hippolyta, as well as the name Philostrate, Theseus' Master of Revels. Additional Theseus material came from Plutarch's life of the hero, as did the names Lysander, Demetrius, and Helena.

A particularly influential source was Ovid's (43 B.C.– A.D. 17?) *Metamorphoses*, the fourth book of which recounts the Pyramus-Thisbe plot that the "rude mechanicals" enact before the courtiers in the final act. (There is about the play, in fact, an especially Ovidian tone in the treatment of the fairies, as well as in the many transformations and metamorphoses through which the characters pass.) By and large, however, these are minor borrowings that in no sense minimize Shakespeare's accomplishment in creating an original and fanciful comedy.

The impending marriage of the Athenian King Theseus to the Amazon Hippolyta constitutes the first thread of plot, one that forms a framing action for the entire play, much as the Aegeon intrigue did for *The Comedy of Errors*. The opening and closing scenes of *A Midsummer Night's Dream* are dominated by the royal couple. Theseus' first-act decree that Hermia must comply with her father's wishes and marry Demetrius, against her will, causes the lovers' plot of Acts II–IV to come about. It is in order to escape the parental and royal edicts that Hermia and Lysander, followed by Demetrius and Helena, flee to the enchanted wood where they fall under the influence of the "watery moon" and the fairies' spell.

It is generally accepted that Shakespeare wrote this comedy in celebration of some noble marriage, although critics cannot agree on exactly which one. Thus, Theseus and Hippolyta serve as surrogates for the noble couple before whom the work is being played. They stand largely outside the action; the events of the plot happen for them, rather than to them. Therefore, after the opening scene we do not see them again until Act IV. They reappear only after all the confusions, transformations, and love madness have been set aright, and they preside over the play-within-a-play of "Pyramus and Thisbe" in Act V. Because *A Midsummer Night's Dream*, like *Love's Labor's Lost*, was played before a courtly audience, the play-within-a-play is once again a royal-entertainment-within-a-royal-entertainment.

The setting of our play, then, is technically ancient Athens, but this is (as in so many of Shakespeare's "period" plays) of little consequence. Their names notwithstanding, the characters are, throughout, thoroughly English. This is especially true of the fairies, whose actions constitute a second major thread of the plot.

The fairies—principally King Oberon, Queen Titania, and Robin Goodfellow (called Puck)—derive from native English folklore. They control the action of the play once it shifts to the enchanted wood, and their activities serve as the adhesive that binds the four subplots together. This is not to say, however, that they lack direct involvement or are themselves immune from magic. Titania—charmed into loving an ignorant weaver with the head of an ass—is as much a victim of enchantment as Lysander and Demetrius. Still, the fairies, particularly Oberon and Puck, exercise almost complete control over the Athenian lovers.

It is precisely because we know that the fairies are in control that we are able to enjoy the confusions and distress of the four lovers: Lysander, Hermia, Demetrius, and Helena. If a supernatural, external force is causing the entanglements, cannot it also untie them? Puck himself assures us, when the love madness is at its most confusing state, that "Jack shall have Jill;/ Nought shall go ill;/The man shall have his mare again, and all shall be well" (III, ii).

Puck is the most purely entertaining of the fairy band. His proper name, from traditional English fairy lore, is Robin Goodfellow, "puck" being a generic term for a mischievous sprite. Robin Goodfellow was known as a tricky but essentially harmless household spirit. At his first entrance, another fairy asks him:

> Are you not he
> That frights the maidens of the villagery;
> Skim milk, and sometimes labour in the quern
> And bootless make the breathless housewife
>   churn;
> And sometime make the drink to bear no barm;
> Mislead night-wanderers, laughing at their
>   harm?

And Puck replies:

> Thou speak'st aright;
> I am that merry wanderer of the night.
> . . . .
> And sometime lurk I in a gossip's bowl,
> In very likeness of a roasted crab,
> And when she drinks, against her lips I bob
> And on her wither'd dewlap pour the ale.
> The wisest aunt, telling the saddest tale,
> Sometime for three-foot stool mistaketh me;
> Then slip I from her bum, down topples she,
> And "tailor" cries, and falls into a cough.
>
> (II, i)

Clearly, Robin Goodfellow evolved in fairy lore as a supernatural explanation for the many trivial mishaps and accidents so commonplace in domestic living.

Puck is instrumental in the movement of the plot. It is he who mistakenly administers the love potion intended for Demetrius to Lysander, thinking him the "disdainful youth" Oberon has described. This sets in motion the love chain of cross-wooings that make up the central action of the comedy. It is also Puck who, out of pure mischief, transforms Bottom into an ass.

In addition to his direct involvement in these plot complications, Puck serves as a *raisonneur*, or chorus figure. He observes the love madness of the Athenians as an outsider and comments on their folly, sometimes directly to the audience and sometimes to them through Oberon:

> Captain of our fairy band,
> Helena is here at hand;
> And the youth, mistook by me,
> Pleading for a lover's fee.
> Shall we their fond pageant see?
> Lord, what fools these mortals be!
>
> (III, ii)

The fairy king Oberon and his consort Titania, unlike Puck, maintain a certain royal bearing and dignity, the exception being Titania's infatuation with the grotesque Bottom. They do not indulge in mischievous trickery, although their magic is potent. We first see them engaged in a jealous quarrel, exchanging accusations of infidelity. This lovers' altercation and their wrangling over possession of the "little changeling boy" precipitate not only the enchantment of the Athenian mortals but also, as Titania states, a "progeny of evils" in the natural world:

> Therefore the winds, piping to us in vain,
> As in revenge, have suck'd up from the sea
> Contagious fogs; which falling in the land
> Have every pelting river made so proud

That they have overborne their continents:
The ox hath therefore stretch'd his yoke in
    vain,
The ploughman lost his sweat, and the green
    corn
Hath rotted ere his youth attain'd a beard;
The fold stands empty in the drowned field,
And crows are fatted with the murrion flock;
. . . .
And thorough this distemperature we see
The seasons alter: hoary-headed frosts
Fall in the fresh lap of the crimson rose,
And on old Hiems' thin and icy crown
An odorous chaplet of sweet summer buds
Is, as in mockery, set: the spring, the summer,
The childing autumn, angry winter, change
Their wonted liveries, and the mazed world,
By their increase, now knows not which is
    which.

                        (II, i)

It is in order to punish and torment Titania that Oberon drops the liquor of the "little western flower" on her eyes, effecting the enchantment that causes her to fall in love with the "translated" Bottom. This flower, the same whose juices Puck mistakenly administers to Lysander, is thematically significant. Oberon tells us that it came into being when Cupid once "loosed his love-shaft smartly from his bow" at a "fair vestal" but missed his target:

Yet mark'd I where the bolt of Cupid fell:
It fell upon a little western flower,
Before milk-white, now purple with love's
    wound,
And maidens call it love-in-idleness.

                        (II, i)

It is the juice of love-in-idleness, then, that afflicts Lysander, Demetrius, and Titania (and indirectly

Hermia, Helena, and Bottom). "Idleness" to the Elizabethans was nearly synonymous with "madness," and
it is love madness that dominates the center of this
comedy. Sudden passion and overwhelming desire
replace rational love, as when Titania dotes on Bottom
or Lysander abruptly switches courtship from one
lady to another.

The antidote to love-in-idleness is the juice of yet
another flower, one that Oberon calls "Dian's bud"
(Diana being, of course, the goddess of chastity).
When this antidote is applied to the eyes of the enchanted, their love madness is dispelled. The night's
"accidents" are remembered by the lovers as but "the
fierce vexation of a dream." Titania, cured of the
"hateful imperfection of her eyes," is reconciled to
Oberon and the two go with their fairy band to bless
the nuptials at the Athenian palace.

The four lovers—and their chaotic night of love in
idleness—constitute the third major thread of action
in the comedy. As in *The Taming of the Shrew* and
The Two Gentlemen of Verona, the source of these
intrigues is Italianate romance (possibly even Montemayor's *Diana*, which inspired *The Two Gentlemen
of Verona*). But in *A Midsummer Night's Dream*,
Shakespeare gave the material the ultimate in complications, making Lysander's prophetic observation
that "the course of true love never did run smooth"
(I, i) the understatement of all time.

Quartets of lovers were to become commonplace in
Shakespeare's comedies (*Much Ado about Nothing*,
Twelfth Night, and *As You Like It*, to name a few),
but we never again find the elaborate variations of
cross-wooing present here in our Athenian quartet. As
the plot develops, we have five distinct states of affairs
in the love intrigues:

1. At some point before the play opens, Demetrius

was betrothed to Helena, and Lysander and Hermia loved each other.

2. As the play opens, Demetrius has shifted his affections and now loves Hermia, as does Lysander. Helena, still in love with Demetrius, is forsaken.

3. In the wood, Puck mistakenly administers the love potion to the sleeping Lysander who awakes, sees Helena, and falls in love with her. Now Lysander loves Helena and Demetrius loves Hermia—the opposite of the original pairing or norm.

4. Oberon administers the potion to Demetrius who, awaking, sees Helena and falls in love with her. Now both Demetrius and Lysander love Helena, and Hermia is forsaken—the reverse of situation 2.

5. Puck administers the antidote to Lysander, who awakes and once more loves Hermia. Demetrius remains in love with Helena, and the original pairings once again prevail, bringing the plot full circle.

It is somewhat atypical of Shakespeare that most of the plot complication is caused by an external force (the juice of love-in-idleness) and that the four lovers are simply ignorant victims, unaware of the cause of their distresses. But the force is a benevolent one, for although it makes the true lover (Lysander) love falsely it also causes the false lover (Demetrius) to return to true love. Upon finally waking and beholding Helena, Demetrius claims:

> To her, my lord,
> Was I betroth'd ere I saw Hermia:
> But, like in sickness, did I loathe this food;
> But, as in health, come to my natural taste,
> Now I do wish it, love it, long for it,
> And will for evermore be true to it.
>
> (IV, i)

Demetrius and Helena are reunited; Theseus consents (for no apparent reason) to the marriage of Lysander and Hermia; and three weddings are celebrated in the fifth act.

Obviously the three threads of action considered thus far reinforce one another in their "nuptials" themes. In addition, the nuptial celebration extends beyond these three marriages to encompass the reconciliation of Oberon and Titania, a kind of remarriage. It is fitting, then, that our fourth thread of action, that of the "rude mechanicals," as Puck calls them, should deal with a love story: "The Most Lamentable Comedy, and Most Cruel Death of Pyramus and Thisbe," enacted by "bully Bottom" and his band.

Shakespeare was undoubtedly well acquainted with the behind-the-scenes activities of amateur theatricals, and his delight in spoofing them is obvious. In the performance by Bottom and the other "hempen homespuns" he gives us a wonderfully entertaining subplot that provides most of the low comedy in *A Midsummer Night's Dream*. So appealing are the mechanicals, in fact, that their plot was (and is, even today) frequently extracted and performed as a playlet in its own right.

An amateur theatrical capped the closing scene of *Love's Labor's Lost*, but with "Pyramus and Thisbe" we enjoy not only the performance (V, i) but also the selection and casting of the script (I, ii) and a rehearsal (III, i), including a hilarious discussion of stage props and settings.

Our amateur Thespians (Bottom the weaver, Quince the carpenter, Snug the joiner, Flute the bellows-mender, Snout the tinker, and Starveling the tailor) choose for their play a love tragedy, a singularly inappropriate choice for a wedding celebration. This "very tragical mirth" of the deaths of Pyramus and Thisbe parodies Shakespeare's own *Romeo and Juliet* (written probably a year earlier) and serves as a ludicrous counterpoint to the love entanglements of *A Midsummer Night's Dream*.

Bottom the weaver is one of Shakespeare's finest clowns and a favorite with audiences whenever the play is performed. His portrait had been lightly sketched before in Launce (*The Two Gentlemen of Verona*) and Costard (*Love's Labor's Lost*). He serves, vis à vis the fairy spells and lovers' fantasies, as a touchstone of prosaic reality. So lacking in creative imagination is this simple weaver that he transmutes the imaginative (the theater) into the hopelessly literal— the reverse of *A Midsummer Night's Dream*'s world. Bottom is the antidote to the dream.

In preparing the play (III, i), Bottom cannot conceive of an audience's ability willingly to suspend its disbelief. He fears that "the ladies cannot abide" Pyramus's killing himself and that the appearance of the lion will be "a most dreadful thing," the terror of which must be allayed by a prologue:

> Nay, you must name his [the actor's] name, and half his face must be seen through the lion's neck: and he himself must speak through, saying thus, or to the same defect,—"Ladies," —or "Fair ladies,—I would wish you,"—or "I would request you,"—or "I would entreat you, —not to fear, not to tremble: my life for yours. . . ." And there indeed let him name his name, and tell them plainly he is Snug the joiner.

The play calls for a moon; Bottom wants to know if the moon will shine the night they play. When Quince assures him that it will, the problem is solved:

> Why, then may you leave a casement of the great chamber window, where we play, open, and the moon may shine in at the casement.

It is Bottom's immunity to imagination that makes his transformation into an ass and subsequent encounter with the Queen of the Fairies so amusing. He is the only mortal in the play who has converse with the fairy world, and it doesn't faze him in the least. When his fellows run away in terror at his "translated" form, he cannot conceive that *he* has changed; it must be a trick on *their* part:

> Why do they run away? This is a knavery of them to make me afeard. . . . I see their knavery: this is to make an ass of me; to fright me, if they could.
>
> (III, i)

He is singularly unimpressed with Titania's overtures of love toward him; he might as well be chatting with the village milkmaid. His introduction to her fairy attendants—Peaseblossom, Cobweb, Moth, and Mustardseed—occasions only some feeble jokes upon their names. They are of use to him only for scratching his hairy face and bringing him some hay. Presented with a unique opportunity to commune with the fairy world, he addresses himself to the supernatural as though it were the commonplace, just as he denigrates the fantasy world of the theater with practical considerations and reality.

It is ironic that Bottom is the only one of the enchanted mortals who remembers his transformation. Upon awaking in the morning (IV, i), the four lovers can barely recall how they came to be in the enchanted wood, but Bottom seems to have a distinct, if unsettling, impression of his "dream":

> I have had a most rare vision. I have had a dream, past the wit of man to say what dream it was: man is but an ass, if he go about to expound this dream. Methought I was—there is no man can tell what. Methought I was,— and methought I had,—but man is but a

> patched fool, if he will offer to say what methought I had.

For Bottom, clearly, the strange is best not tampered with.

The language of *A Midsummer Night's Dream* is richly varied and laden with imagery. The dialogue of its royal personages—Theseus, Hippolyta, Oberon, and Titania—is blank verse, although Oberon speaks in rhyme when discussing magical subjects. Puck's spells are cast in a sing-song verse form, usually trochaic tetrameter. Nearly all of the Athenian lovers' lines are rhymed, occasionally quite artificially so. The effect of this, especially at the height of enchantment and cross-wooing, is to prevent us from taking matters too seriously. The mechanicals speak prose, but their playlet is cast in doggerel and sing-song rhymes that parody medieval romance.

A Midsummer Night's Dream represents Shakespeare's initial achievement, in comedy, in creating and sustaining patterns of poetic imagery that enhance the meaning and mood of the play. Although the subject of imagery here deserves extended treatment, a single example must suffice.

Beginning with the opening scene, an image cluster based upon eyes, looking, and seeing is established. Loving Demetrius against her father's will, Hermia protests, "I would my father look'd but with my eyes," to which Theseus replies, "Rather your eyes must with his judgement look." Later in the scene, Hermia despairs of her father's preference for Lysander: "O hell! to choose love by another's eyes." Helena describes Hermia's eyes as "lode-stars." And Hermia tells Lysander that they must "from Athens turn away our eyes" and "starve our sight/From lovers' food till morrow deep midnight." This eye imagery continues throughout the play in various forms. According to a count by Ralph Berry, the word "eye" (including compounds and plurals) occurs sixty-eight times in the play, "see" is used thirty-nine times, and "sight" appears ten times.[1]

The eye imagery suggests and reinforces thematic concerns about love, the principal subject of the comedy. Put most simply, "Love is blind." But on a more complex level, the eyes are treated as the betrayers of judgment and of the rational. Conventionally, of course, love enters through the eyes, but in this comedy it is usually false love—love-in-idleness. Potions and antidotes are squeezed onto the eyes of the sleepers, causing them to see "with parted eye,/ When every thing seems double" (IV, i). Even Titania cannot "see" how ugly Bottom is.

In the first four acts of this comedy, love is a disordered condition of the imagination—a sort of romantic astigmatism. It is so, of course, because the flight to the wood and its fairy world is a retreat from the rational and ordered world of the Athenian court, where parental and societal authority prevails. When morning comes and all the characters return to Athens, order is again restored and each lover returns to the correct beloved. Each lover now "sees" clearly. It is largely through the use of imagery like this that Shakespeare embodied in the language of *A Midsummer Night's Dream* its thematic concerns about love, natural order, rational judgment, and creative fantasy.

Possibly because of its intense appeal to the imagination, *A Midsummer Night's Dream* has been one of Shakespeare's more successful comedies on the stage, particularly in modern times. It was fashionable in the seventeenth and eighteenth centuries to play the work in adapted form. A 1661 version, for example, utilized only the mechanicals' plot, as a "droll" or light entertainment called "The Merry Conceited Humours of Bottom the Weaver." David Garrick turned *A Midsummer Night's Dream* into a full-scale opera in 1755, with some twenty songs and with lavish scenic spectacle.

Shakespeare's original text was more or less restored to the stage by Charles Mathews in his 1840 production, the one that introduced Felix Mendelssohn's famous overture to the play. Other notable nineteenth-century mountings of the comedy were those of Samuel Phelps (who played Bottom) at Sadler's Wells in 1853, of Augustin Daly in New York in 1887, and of F. R. Benson in 1889. All of these productions, typical of their time, emphasized lavish scenic spectacle, pageantry, and music in an attempt to render Shakespeare's extravagant fantasy through concrete, visual opulence of the most literal kind.

In our own century there have been two productions worth noting here for their opposing approaches to the realm of poetic fantasy. Max Reinhardt staged the play a number of times, leading to his 1935 film version for Warner Brothers. Reinhardt, in both the stage and the film versions, took literalism as far as it could go, trusting nothing to the imagination. Dozens of gossamer fairies with glittering wings skipped about on golden moonbeams, through a lush and detailed forest to an Athenian palace rivaling the Parthenon. Unfortunately, much of Shakespeare's text was cut and what poetry remained seemed only to interfere with the visual effects. Reinhardt was as scrupulous in his approach to the magic of *A Midsummer Night's Dream* as Bottom was in rendering the true tragedy of Pyramus and Thisbe.

The other version earned world-wide critical acclaim as a breakthrough in Shakespearean stage production. It was staged by Peter Brook for the Royal Shakespeare Company at Stratford-upon-Avon in 1970

Peter Brook's famous production of *A Midsummer Night's Dream* for the Royal Shakespeare Company, 1970. Watching Titania (Sara Kestelman) and Bottom (David Waller) in their feathery "bower" are Oberon (Alan Howard) and Puck (John Kane). Directed by Peter Brook; designed by Sally Jacobs.

and subsequently toured America. Brook stripped away all preconceived notions about fairies and fantasy, throwing out production tradition accumulated over some three hundred years, and rendered his Athenian world in singularly Spartan terms. His setting was a pure white rectangular room with cushions for the actors to sit upon and ropes and trapezes for them to climb; his lighting was white, bright, and constant; his fairies wore uniforms suggesting jogging suits; and supernatural effects were replaced by full emphasis upon the actors' voices and bodily movements, which included calisthenics and gymnastics.

Through the visual austerity and actor-centered focus of his production, Brook was able to redirect the audience's attention to Shakespeare's text—to its lyricism, its imagery, its fantasy. Therein lay his success. If there is magic in *A Midsummer Night's Dream* (and decidedly there is), it is the magic not of let's-pretend sprites prancing about in gauze-and-glitter fairy suits, but of the English language, raised by the fertile imagination of its greatest poet to full suggestive power.

The Merchant of Venice

In 1594 one Dr. Roderigo Lopez, a Portuguese Jew and physician to Queen Elizabeth, was executed in London—hanged, drawn, and quartered before a cheering crowd for supposed treason against the Queen. The incident caused a flurry of antialien and anti-Semite activity among Londoners, including an enormously successful revival of Marlowe's *The Jew of Malta* at the Rose. It is not surprising, then, that Shakespeare, in 1596 or 1597, came up with a rival Jew play, *The Merchant of Venice*.

This play consolidates two principal lines of action: the "pound of flesh" involvement of Antonio and Shylock, and the "casket" plot, in which Bassanio wins the hand and fortune of Portia. Both actions derive from earlier sources and, as usual, Shakespeare was masterful in combining them.

A fourteenth-century Italian novella, *Il Pecorone*, published in 1558, served as the source for the story of the Jewish usurer who entraps a Venetian merchant into pledging a pound of his own flesh as security for a loan. This same novella provides a lady of Belmont (Shakespeare's Portia) who appears disguised in court to defend the merchant, as well as the ring-exchange business that dominates Shakespeare's fifth act.

The other source is a story in the *Gesta Romanorum*, a fourteenth-century collection of medieval tales, which closely parallels Shakespeare's handling of the lover's test: the choosing between three caskets made of gold, silver, and lead.

The Merchant of Venice represents an abrupt break in the chain of happy romantic plots that Shakespeare had been forging in his five previous comedies. The serious tone of its action borders on the tragic, prefiguring the later so-called problem plays, like *Measure for Measure* and *All's Well That Ends Well*. Its first four acts, dominated by the bond of the pound of flesh, seem to propel its antagonists Shylock and Antonio toward a tragic catastrophe. True, Shakespeare frequently had introduced serious complications into his comedies, but always with the comforting assurance that "all shall be well." In *The Merchant of Venice* there is no Oberon with magical powers to assure us, early in the plot, of a happy denouement. The reversal of the potentially tragic action comes in the person of Portia, in the great courtroom scene (IV, i), but we are given no previous notice— no dramatic preparation—that this will occur.

Moreover, this "comedy" is almost devoid of laughter, and its infrequent attempts at broad comedy pale in comparison with what Shakespeare had achieved earlier and was to achieve again. Its single clown figure, Launcelot Gobbo, is but a poor echo of Launce in *The Two Gentlemen of Verona* or Costard in *Love's Labor's Lost*. H. B. Charlton called him "the slenderest and most pointlessly fatuous of Shakespeare's clowns."[1]

Even more disturbing than this comedy's lack of conventional comic material is the ambiguity of its action. Critics and commentators can reach no consensus as to Shakespeare's thematic intent, nor can they agree on any clearcut interpretations of the play's complex and fascinating characters, especially Shylock the Jew.

In approaching *The Merchant of Venice*, the reader will benefit from an awareness of the traditional attitudes of Elizabethans toward Jews and usury. Since the reign of Edward I, Jews had been legally excluded from England, and those few who were allowed were expected to convert outwardly to Christianity. Thus, a Jew was to an Elizabethan a quite exotic figure—a foreigner and an infidel. The average London theater-goer (who had probably never seen a Jew) undoubtedly took Marlowe's characterization of Barabas—a ranting, bloodthirsty villain—as representative.

The interpretation of Shylock, upon which readers, critics, directors, and actors will never agree, is the crux of the play. John Dover Wilson called it the "most baffling character-problem, after that of Hamlet, in Shakespeare."[2] In the theater, the character has been played as everything from a ludicrous clown (Thomas Dogget in 1701) to a dignified and aristocratic, although malevolent, martyr (Henry Irving in 1879). Shakespeare seems intentionally to have created this ambiguity, for we are never certain of the degree of villainy that we are to attach to the character. He is by turns a ruthless usurer, a wronged father, a bloodthirsty Christian-hater, and a pathetic victim of the loathing heaped upon him by the "good" Christians of the piece.

Usury, the practice by which Shylock makes his living, is condemned in the Bible and was officially renounced in Shakespeare's England. It was considered abhorrent to the Elizabethans that money should breed money, and Shylock's pride in making it do so, even more than his religion perhaps, marked him as a villainous character to the average theatergoer.

Nevertheless, as a dramatic villain in the vein of Barabas, Shylock is, fortunately, a failure. He does not resemble even Shakespeare's other villains (Richard III, Iago, *King Lear*'s Edmund, Iachimo), for he is largely without cunning or deception. Shylock never deceives anyone, nor do the other characters have any illusions about him. From the first, Antonio calls him a devil and Bassanio speaks of his "villain's mind" (I, iii); Launcelot Gobbo, his servant, leaves him because he is "the very devil incarnal" (II, ii); and the Venetian Christians openly revile him.

Conventional villains commit evil deeds chiefly because it pleases them to do so; Shylock's cruelty to Antonio, although indefensible, is a well-motivated response to the abuse and indignity that Antonio and the others heap upon him. From the outset, Shylock makes clear his feelings toward Antonio and his reasons for them:

> I hate him for he is a Christian,
> But more for that in low simplicity
> He lends out money gratis and brings down
> The rate of usance here with us in Venice.
> . . . .
> He hates our sacred nation, and he rails,
> Even there where merchants most do congre-
>   gate,
> On me, my bargains and my well-won thrift,
> Which he calls interest.
>
>   (I, iii)

Later, when Shylock is determined to foreclose on the bond and have his pound of flesh, Antonio confesses to Salarino:

> He seeks my life; his reason well I know:
> I oft deliver'd from his forfeitures
> Many that have at times made moan to me;
> Therefore he hates me.
>
>   (III, iii)

Clearly, Antonio is not content merely to despise the Jew; he would deny Shylock his very livelihood.

The enmity between the two is palpable. In Act I, scene iii, Antonio insults Shylock to his face:

> An evil soul producing holy witness
> Is like a villain with a smiling cheek,
> A goodly apple rotten at the heart.

Their feud has existed long before the play begins. In response to Antonio's request for the loan of three thousand ducats, Shylock counters:

> Signior Antonio, many a time and oft
> In the Rialto you have rated me
> About my moneys and my usances:
> Still have I borne it with a patient shrug,
> For sufferance is the badge of all our tribe.
> You call me misbeliever, cut-throat dog,
> And spit upon my Jewish gaberdine,
> And all for use of that which is mine own.

—to which Antonio replies:

> I am as like to call thee so again,
> To spit on thee again, to spurn thee too.

This "villainous" Jew is more than amply motivated.

The problem of interpreting Shylock is further complicated by Shakespeare's having endowed the character with keen feelings that arouse our sympathy. Although we hate the act he would perform, we cannot hate the man. The havoc that the Christians wreak upon his life culminates in the loss of his only daughter Jessica, who elopes with a gentile (Lorenzo), renounces her faith, and ransacks her father's house for all the money she can lay her hands on. It is after suffering this blow that Shylock determines to exact the pound of flesh from the defaulting Antonio. His losses cruelly mocked by the vicious Salanio and Salarino, he responds with one of Shakespeare's great arguments for humane understanding:

> Hath not a Jew eyes? hath not a Jew hands, organs, dimensions, senses, affections, passions? fed with the same food, hurt with the same weapons, subject to the same diseases, healed by the same means, warmed and cooled by the same winter and summer, as a Christian is? If you prick us, do we not bleed? if you tickle us, do we not laugh? if you poison us, do we not die? and if you wrong us, shall we not revenge?
>
> (III, i)

In this speech Shakespeare shows us a Shylock capable of profound hurt and at the same time sets the stage for his vengeful cruelty at the trial. He is not precisely "a man more sinned against than sinning," but his thirst for Antonio's blood is fully comprehensible to us.

Perhaps the best solution to the enigma of Shylock is that advanced by H. B. Charlton,[3] who proposed that Shakespeare set out to "let the Jew dog have it" by creating a thoroughly despicable villain, frankly catering to his audience's (and most likely his own) anti-Semitic inclinations. Here the dramatist failed, said Charlton, because his artist's sensibility and feeling for truth balked at the creation of a reprehensible stereotype and led him instead to depict a fully motivated and often sympathetic member of the human community. C. L. Barber viewed the character similarly: "Shakespeare's marvelous creative sympathy takes the stock role of Jewish usurer and villain and conveys how it would feel to be a man living inside it."[4]

Of course, any interpretation of Shylock is impossible without a consideration of the figures who play against him (and there is not a single character, except Tubal, who plays *with* him), especially Antonio and Portia. Unfortunately, the Venetians are as ambiguous as the Jew. They have been characterized by some critics as noble, loving Christians who mercifully convert the Jew to Christianity, and by others as cold-hearted wasters and rotters. (The latter view is expressed in the introduction by Sir Arthur Quiller-Couch to the New Cambridge edition.)

What are we to make of Antonio, the merchant for whom this play is named? He is Shylock's chief antagonist but seems ill-suited to the role. He opens the comedy with, "In sooth, I know not why I am so sad," and remains largely melancholy, passive, and detached to the end. As an adversary to Shylock in the courtroom he is strangely resigned to defeat, indicating no fewer than five times his readiness—almost eagerness—to die. It is only Portia's intervention that saves him, and he has little to say by way of thanks. He borders on the petulant.

Antonio's love for Bassanio, emphasized throughout, is so strong as to lead him to sacrifice his life for his friend. This is within the tradition of "amity" or male friendship, a convention that is central also to *The Two Gentlemen of Verona*. What is unique here, however, is that all the proofs of friendship, as well as the intended sacrifice, are one-sided. Bassanio uses his friend to gain financing for his romantic venture, then goes off a-courting to Belmont, leaving Antonio to answer for the pound of flesh. Antonio seems almost to find pleasure in being thus abused.

The typical lover's quartet in Shakespeare's comedies involves a pair of friends or blood relations (either male or female), each of whom finds a mate at the comedy's conclusion—Valentine and Proteus, Lysander and Demetrius, Kate and Bianca, and so on. Typically, then, Antonio should perform in the love quartet,

considering his attachment to Bassanio, but his part is
played by the abrasive Gratiano. It is Gratiano who
wins Nerissa in the third act and supplies the last act
with its merry and bawdy humor. Antonio watches
the festivity from the sidelines.

It is strange that Antonio, a young, noble figure who
inspires the admiring comments of all in Venice, is
given no romantic interest whatever. In the courtroom,
he responds to Bassanio's cheery encouragement with:

> I am a tainted wether of the flock,
> Meetest for death: the weakest kind of fruit
> Drops earliest to the ground; and so let me.
>
> (IV, i)

A wether is a castrated ram. Antonio is, for dramatic
purposes, asexual. Our merchant of Venice is a loser,
and there is something almost pathological in his behavior—from his opening melancholy, through his
resignation to death, to his final detachment from the
general merriment.

The other major character who functions in opposition to Shylock is Portia, the heiress of Belmont.
She is the central figure in the "casket" plot and the
one who brings the two story lines together. Although
less ambiguous than Shylock and Antonio, she is no
less intriguing as a dramatic character. She exists
almost in a world apart from the Venetians. Her single
appearance in Venice and sole contact with Shylock is
in the courtroom scene, where she is disguised as a
man. Her plea to Shylock ("The quality of mercy is
not strained . . .") is one of the more famous speeches
in Shakespeare, and her role has long been a favorite
with actresses.

Shakespeare seems to have drawn in Portia a
portrait of ideal womanhood. She is first described by
Bassanio:

In Belmont is a lady richly left;
And she is fair and, fairer than that word,
Of wondrous virtues: sometimes from her eyes
I did receive fair speechless messages:
Her name is Portia, nothing undervalued
To Cato's daughter, Brutus' Portia:
Nor is the wide world ignorant of her worth,
For the four winds blow in from every coast
Renowned suitors, and her sunny locks
Hang on her temples like a golden fleece;
Which makes her seat of Belmont Colchos'
    strand,
And many Jasons come in quest of her.

(I, i)

Of course the fellow is in love with her, but what he says turns out to be fairly accurate. In the very next scene we see this paragon of "wondrous virtues" discussing with her maid Nerissa the "renowned suitors" who have lately sought her hand: a Neapolitan prince, a count Palatine, a French lord, an English baron, a Scottish lord, and a German duke. True to her late father's wishes, she must dismiss them all for refusing to choose among the three caskets—the lover's test.

When Bassanio arrives at Belmont to take the casket test, she will not break her oath to her departed father, even though she admits her strong preference for the handsome Venetian:

I could teach you
How to choose right, but I am then forsworn;
So will I never be: so may you miss me;
But if you do, you'll make me wish a sin,
That I had been forsworn.

(III, ii)

Her generosity becomes apparent when, upon learning of Antonio's predicament, she offers to bail him out:

> PORTIA. What sum owes he the Jew?
> BASSANIO. For me three thousand ducats.
> PORTIA.   What, no more?
>   Pay him six thousand, and deface the bond;
>   Double six thousand, and then treble that,
>   Before a friend of this description
>   Shall lose a hair through Bassanio's fault.
>   . . . .
>   You shall have gold
>   To pay the petty debt twenty times over.
>
>   (III, ii)

In all her dealings, Portia's integrity, generosity, and noble spirit are evident.

Portia's appearance in the courtroom comes as a complete surprise to the audience—a most unusual piece of dramaturgy for Shakespeare. At the end of Act III, scene iv, we learn that she and Nerissa are to disguise themselves as men and go to Venice, but no mention is made of the nature of the disguise or of their purpose in donning it. Portia tells her maid merely that "I have work in hand/That you yet know not of," and that "I'll tell thee all my whole device/When I am in my coach." Although transvestite disguise is standard Shakespeare fare, never was it employed with such a total lack of justification. It is justified in retrospect, of course. The audience immediately recognizes the lawyer "Balthasar" as Portia, even though the Venetians do not.

The courtroom scene (IV, i) is the climax of the play, and it is one of Shakespeare's finest. It counterposes two basic concerns in human conduct: justice and mercy. Shylock has the law on his side, embracing a sort of Old Testament eye-for-an-eye sense of justice. It is made quite clear that the court and even the Duke are powerless to save Antonio without arbitrarily setting aside the laws of Venice and toppling the whole structure of civil conduct. Even Portia recognizes this:

> It must not be; there is no power in Venice
> Can alter a decree established:
> 'Twill be recorded for a precedent,
> And many an error by the same example
> Will rush into the state: it cannot be.

Portia's only argument in Antonio's behalf is to ask Shylock for mercy, in the New Testament sense of Christian charity. Mercy is "an attribute to God himself," for without God's mercy (grace) "none of us/ Should see salvation." But Shylock will have none of that Christian cant and insists on the absolute letter of the law, honing his knife in preparation.

In all, Portia makes three appeals to Shylock, attempting to touch him on three different levels, from the most spiritual to the most corporeal. The "quality of mercy" speech advocates mercy as a spiritual attribute. Next she appeals to his love of worldly goods by asking him to "take thrice thy money" instead of the flesh, and again Shylock refuses. The third appeal is at the basic level of human feeling and physical empathy:

> Have by some surgeon, Shylock, on your
>   charge,
> To stop his wounds, lest he do bleed to death.
> . . . .
> 'Twere good you do so much for charity.

But Shylock is without charity where Antonio is concerned.

There is wonderful irony throughout this scene. Portia, after each failure to move Shylock, reaffirms his legal right to proceed with the butchery. Each time she does so, he praises her impartiality and wisdom:

> A Daniel come to judgement! yea, a Daniel!
> O wise young judge, how I do honour thee!
> . . . .
> O noble judge! O excellent young man!
> . . . .
>   O wise and upright judge!
> How much more elder art thou than thy looks!
> . . . .
> Most rightful judge!
> . . . .
> Most learned judge! A sentence! Come,
>   prepare!

His fawning admiration for the judge reaches a climax in this last line, and it is followed immediately by Portia's "Tarry a little; there is something else." Then the tables turn on Shylock. Portia cites the Venetian law that will provide for confiscation of his goods "if thou dost shed/One drop of Christian blood." Moreover, a second law provides for death to any alien who attempts to take the life of a Venetian. (It is an absurdity, of course, that the Duke and Magnificoes of Venice would not have been familiar with these laws all along, but the dramatic power of the moment conceals the flaw in logic.) Shylock is thwarted in his revenge, dispossessed of his wealth, and forced to convert to Christianity. Now it is the coarse-grained Gratiano who mockingly cries, and more than once, "A second Daniel, a Daniel, Jew!"

Because there is no dramatic preparation for Portia's appearance in the courtroom, and because she appears in male attire, she becomes almost a different character than the romantic, girlish heiress of Belmont. It is as though Shakespeare had conceived of her here in more universal terms. Her judicial acumen, her masculine bearing, her wisdom—all serve to embody in her an omniscient external force. Perhaps she is a dramatic surrogate for divine intercession. She assumes a similar role briefly in the fifth act where, having rescued Antonio's body, she again plays the deus ex machina and rescues his fortune:

> Antonio, you are welcome;
> And I have better news in store for you
> Than you expect: unseal this letter soon;
> There you shall find three of your argosies
> Are richly come to harbour suddenly:
> You shall not know by what strange accident
> I chanced on this letter.
>
> (V, i)

Strange accident indeed! Antonio can respond only with, "I am dumb."

It is true that Portia is technically only the reporter of this miraculous bit of good fortune, but the dramatic effect is that she is the author of it. (A careful reader, although certainly not an auditor, might ask how she knows what was in the letter, since it is still sealed.) The suggestion of omniscience is unmistakable.

Were it not for its fifth act, *The Merchant of Venice* would hardly qualify as a comedy. The story of the play is fully told by the end of the fourth act, and the only plot element to carry over to the final act is the rather trivial merriment over the forfeited rings.

This ring business, though seemingly extraneous, can be related thematically to the Shylock plot. In taunting her lord for breaking his oath never to remove her ring, Portia serves, at the level of festivity, as a Shylock exacting his just due. Bassanio has forfeited a lover's bond in giving the ring to the barrister (the disguised Portia), and it is only the power of Portia's love—her mercy—that sets aside the legalism of justice and cancels the debt. Frank Kermode has called this final act a "thematic appendix to the dramatic action."[5]

The fifth act serves also to erase the unpleasantness of the tragicomic Shylock plot through its light lyricism and its miraculous restoration of Antonio's argosies. It contains some of the finest poetry in the play, particularly in the lyrical exchange between Lorenzo and Jessica in celebration of the night. Through its moonlit night and its ever-present music—Shakespeare's recurrent symbol of harmony—this final scene at Belmont puts the troubled Venetian world to rest:

> The Fifth Act redeems us into a world in which good folk are happy with free hearts that move to music, without an understanding of which a man is fit only for treasons, stratagems and spoils. We have to be won back to a saner, happier acceptance of life; and so we are, by gracious, most playful comedy.[6]

The stage history of *The Merchant of Venice* is virtually a history of the changing approaches to Shylock; most great actors have at some time or another undertaken this tempting role. In a 1701 adaptation called *The Jew of Venice*, the Restoration comedian Thomas Dogget rendered Shakespeare's Jew as a ludicrous villain, a view that did not change significantly until Charles Macklin's 1741 production at Drury Lane. Macklin endowed Shylock with considerable malevolence, but with tender feeling as well. It was one of the earliest efforts to play any Shakespeare text as it was written, and it was so successful that Macklin continued to play his Shylock for nearly fifty years.

Edmund Kean made his triumphant Drury Lane debut as Shylock in 1814, and Sir Henry Irving had

Bassanio (Mark Lamos, left) quiets Gratiano (Kenneth Welsh) in the 1973 production of *The Merchant of Venice* at the Guthrie Theater, Minneapolis. Production directed by Michael Langham; costumes by Sam Kirkpatrick; scenery by Eoin Sprott.

COURTESY OF THE GUTHRIE THEATER, MINNEAPOLIS

great success with the role in 1879, subsequently touring America with it. Other great English Shylocks have included Richard Burbage (the original), John Philip Kemble, Samuel Phelps, Charles Macready, Johnston

Forbes-Robertson, Sir Herbert Beerbohm Tree, and, in a successful Victorian-dress version at London's Old Vic in 1970, Sir Laurence Olivier.

The Merchant of Venice was the first play produced in America by Lewis Hallam at Williamsburg, Virginia, in 1752. Many great American actors have since played the Jew, notably Edwin Booth, Otis Skinner, and Walter Hampden. The complexities of Shylock and the charms of Portia continue to make *The Merchant of Venice* one of the more popular of Shakespeare's plays in the modern theater.

The Merry Wives of Windsor

Tradition has it—and critics have found no good reason to dispute it—that Shakespeare wrote *The Merry Wives of Windsor* at the express command of his sovereign. Good Queen Bess, the story goes, was so taken with the character of Sir John Falstaff in the *Henry IV* chronicle plays that she instructed the playwright to produce a comedy of "Falstaff in love"—and to produce it "within a Fortnight." If this be so, it goes a long way toward explaining some of the peculiar features of this most un-Shakespearean of Shakespeare's comedies.

To begin with, the play is unique in the Shakespeare comic canon for offering a fairly realistic, unpoetic portrait of middle-class life in an English country town. As such, it lacks the exotic settings (Verona, Athens, Venice) and elevated personages (the Duke of Milan, the King of Navarre, Theseus and Hippolyta) of the romantic tales typically told in Shakespeare's comedies. Its characters are plain Mr. and Mrs. It lacks also the lyricism with which Shakespeare traditionally told such tales. *The Merry Wives of Windsor* is singularly prosaic; the bulk of its dialogue (about 85 percent) is cast in earthy, colloquial prose. What little verse it has is poor by Shakespeare standards and appears mainly in Fenton's wooing of Anne Page and in the fairy masque of the final scene.

Uncharacteristic, too, is the comedy's total freedom from seriousness or any threat of harm. Even *The Comedy of Errors* had its Aegeon being led off to execution, but the most threatening element in *The Merry Wives of Windsor* is Ford's obsessive jealousy over his wife. And even jealousy is comic here; Ford is no Othello, no Leontes.

There is no way of knowing if Shakespeare met the putative two-week deadline in pulling together the diverse elements of his comedy. But the work does show signs of haste, carelessness, and disregard of detail, whatever its attractiveness at the level of merry farce. To expedite his task, he may have drawn upon an earlier play in his company's repertory, *The Jealous Comedy* (now lost), as a source for his plot. But whatever the source, the story elements of *The Merry Wives of Windsor* are common props in the trunk of theatrical playmaking.

There are two principal lines of action in this comedy, joined structurally in the last act and related thematically throughout. The main interest is the repeated duping of Falstaff by the "merry wives": Mrs. Ford and Mrs. Page. The underplot concerns the wooing of the latter's daughter, "sweet Anne Page," by the silly Slender, the French doctor Caius, and the poor but honest Fenton. The theme of both plots—if one would ponder themes in the midst of merriment—is the triumph of homespun honesty over mercenary double-dealing.

In combining the two lines of action, Shakespeare created a complex plot of no fewer than eleven separate intrigues, or "practices," by character(s) against character(s). Unfortunately, not all the separate intrigues are essential to the whole, nor are all the details carefully worked out.

The comedy begins, for example, with Justice Shallow's accusation that Falstaff has "beaten my men, killed my deer, and broke open my lodge" (I, i), a matter so grave that Shallow will "make a Star-chamber matter of it." The matter comes to naught, however; by the third scene Falstaff is off on his courtship of the merry wives, and Shallow's complaint is never mentioned again. Similarly, the Host of the Garter is cheated and robbed of his horses by some German confidence men (IV, v), but the business is dropped—a pointless irrelevancy. Ford asks the Host (II, i) to present him in disguise to Falstaff as "Master Brook," but when the presentation takes place (II, ii) it is Bardolph who makes the introduction. Finally, it is established no fewer than three times (IV, iv; IV, vi; V, iii) that Anne Page will enact the Fairy Queen in Windsor Park, but when the fairies appear (V, v) Mistress Quickly has inexplicably become Queen of the Fairies.[1] Such inconsistencies occur throughout the comedy.

Critics have varied in their appraisals of *The Merry Wives of Windsor.* Most have found fault with the play, not so much on its own terms as in its tenuous and confusing relationship to the *Henry IV* plays, especially since the character of Sir John Falstaff appears in both parts of *Henry IV* as well as in *The Merry Wives of Windsor.* The problem of relating the three plays is additionally complicated by the inability of scholars to determine exactly when the comedy was written. Estimates have ranged from 1592 to 1601, and attempts to fit its composition into the sequence of *1 Henry IV, 2 Henry IV,* and *Henry V* have failed. (The death of Falstaff is reported in *Henry V.*)

It is perhaps best to conclude that Shakespeare had no intention of making *The Merry Wives of Windsor* fit chronologically or historically into the scheme of the Henry plays, or of relating the biographical details of this Falstaff to the Falstaff of the chronicles. His assignment being a comedy of "Falstaff in love," he could hardly alter the name Falstaff, even though he created in the comedy a character wholly inconsistent with what he had produced in the histories. The inconsistency, which most critics have seized on, centers on what is generally referred to as "the degradation of Falstaff" in *The Merry Wives of Windsor*.

The object of this degradation is, in the *Henry IV* plays, one of Shakespeare's finest comic creations. He is a corpulent but energetic figure who invariably turns every occasion to his own advantage. A thief, rogue, liar, and sometime coward, he nevertheless arouses our full sympathy and admiration for his quick wit and continual besting of his fellows—even of Prince Hal.

The Sir John of *The Merry Wives of Windsor* is a dim-witted and cowardly buffoon by comparison. He alone is successfully deceived by all (Pistol, Nym, Ford, Mrs. Ford, Mrs. Page, Mistress Quickly, and others) and deceives no one. He may resemble the Falstaff of the histories in his girth ["I am in the waist two yards about" (I, iii)], in an occasional speech of characteristic bravado (see, for example, III, v), and in intermittent flashes of witty wordplay, but he is chiefly a gull and a contemptuous figure in the eyes of his fellows—a patsy without even the common sense to realize that he is being taken. True, he provides much of the play's mirth, but we laugh derisively at him, not with him.

In a sense, Shakespeare ducked his assignment, for we never see Falstaff "in love." "Lechery" might serve as an apt term, but even his intended seduction of the two wives is a mercenary matter. His eye is on their husbands' coffers, as he readily admits: "I will be cheater to them both, and they shall be exchequers to me; they shall be my East and West Indies, and I will trade to them both" (I, iii). He tells Ford to his face, thinking him to be Master Brook, of his intention to seduce his (Ford's) wife:

> They say the jealous wittolly knave hath masses of money; for the which his wife seems to me well-favoured. I will use her as the key of the cuckoldly rogue's coffer; and there's my harvest-home.
>
> (II, ii)

Falstaff has not a chance of succeeding in his mercenary mission, as Shakespeare failed to endow him with much common sense. He sends identical love letters to both women, knowing full well that they are best friends and are sure to compare notes. His subsequent failure to perceive that the wives are deliberately tricking him is even more incredible. After being carried off in a buck-basket and dumped in the Thames, he comes back for more, only to be beaten and reduced to an ignominious escape in women's clothing. If this is "Falstaff in love," one is tempted to second H. B. Charlton's claim that *The Merry Wives of Windsor* is a "cynical revenge which Shakespeare took on the hitherto unsuspecting gaiety of his own creative exuberance."[2]

The degradation of Falstaff is completed in the final scene. Terrified at the approach of the "fairies," he falls face down to the ground and submits to being pinched and burned by a band of children, howling all the while. When the torment ends and the mock fairies are unmasked, how does he acquit himself?

> And these are not fairies? I was three or four times in the thought they were not fairies: and yet the guiltiness of my mind, the sudden sur-

> prise of my powers, drove the grossness of the
> foppery into a received belief, in despite of
> the teeth of all rhyme and reason, that they
> were fairies.

This craven dimwit is certainly not the Falstaff of *Henry IV*.

The connection to the chronicle plays does not rest with Falstaff alone, for Shakespeare chose to include among his dramatis personae a number of other characters who figured in the Henry plays: Justice Shallow, Bardolph, Nym, Pistol, and Mistress Quickly. The four male characters are mere shadows of their former selves, having little to do in the plot and serving only as amusing eccentrics. Nym is said to exemplify (or perhaps satirize) the "humours" character, a comic type with a single dominant trait. The convention of humours characterization was developed in the comedies of Ben Jonson around 1600, and Shakespeare may have been spoofing the convention with Nym, who uses the word "humour" in nearly every speech—twenty-one times in all.

Mistress Quickly, a minor character in the *Henry IV* plays, becomes a major figure in *The Merry Wives of Windsor* and a source of great fun. She, too, differs from her histories' counterpart, but the changes are for the good. She is the only character in the play who is fully aware of all of the intrigues. Indeed, she is involved in most of them. As go-between for the three suitors to Anne Page, she serves all three, although she admits a preference for Fenton. She is also go-between and confidante for the merry wives and engineers the duping of Falstaff. (Strangely enough, she has never before met Falstaff in this play, even though the two were intimate in *Henry IV*.) As Fairy Queen, she oversees Falstaff's final degradation in Windsor Park.

All in all, she is the most functional character in the plot.

She is also one of the most entertaining. Her frequent malapropisms ("allicholy" for "melancholy," "canary" for "quandary," "fartuous" for "virtuous," and so on) put her in the company of some of Shakespeare's better clowns: Costard, Dogberry, Bottom, and others. She is perfectly ingenuous and seems incapable of making moral distinctions. She proceeds in all her dealings under the assumption that people are good. It bothers her not a whit that she is employed to advance the suits of three competing wooers to Anne Page; she gives each her best effort:

> I would my master [Caius] had Mistress Anne; or I would Master Slender had her; or, in sooth, I would Master Fenton had her: I will do what I can for them all three; for so I have promised, and I'll be as good as my word; but speciously for Master Fenton.
>
> (III, iv)

John Dover Wilson recognized the special charm of this Mistress Quickly and ventured an opinion as to why she has so frequently been slighted in criticism. It is a telling comment on critical attitudes toward the comedy in general:

> She is surely one of the most precious characters in all Shakespeare, and would long ago have been recognized as such, had not the whole play . . . been overshadowed and obscured by the silly debate about the degradation of Falstaff.[3]

The Merry Wives of Windsor is peopled with minor characters whose sole mission it is to delight us; none is developed at any length. "Sweet Anne Page" is simply sweetness. She exists largely outside the intrigues of the plot, a catalyst rather than a participant. Her innocence and sincerity make her worthy of Fenton's love, and we forgive her for marrying him against her parents' wishes. After all, Doctor Caius and Slender court Anne for mercenary reasons, "where there was no proportion held in love" (V, v). Fenton embodies true love: "He capers, he dances, he has eyes of youth, he writes verses, he speaks holiday, he smells April and May" (III, ii).

Sir Hugh Evans, the Welsh parson, and Doctor Caius, the French physician, are one-joke figures. Their thick accents and abuse of the English language play at the level of music-hall burlesque; characters who speak in dialect traditionally invite ridicule. Their intended jealous duel over Anne, which never materializes, is one of the comedy's abortive intrigues that lead nowhere, and the two end up friends.

The Merry Wives of Windsor ends, like *Love's Labor's Lost* and *A Midsummer Night's Dream*, in masquelike festivity, again attesting to the likelihood of performance at Court. The singing and dancing of the "urchins, ouphes, and fairies" at Windsor Park insures the final humiliation of Falstaff, but it also undoubtedly provided the performing children of Windsor, favorites of the Queen, with an opportunity to entertain their sovereign. They function much like the fairies at the end of *A Midsummer Night's Dream* —a supernatural force that sets all aright—as they provide the correction of Falstaff and facilitate the elopement of Fenton and Anne. Unlike the fairies of *A Midsummer Night's Dream*, they are not literally supernatural beings, but the effect dramatically is the same.

Not all critics have been impressed with the merriment of *The Merry Wives of Windsor*. Charlton saw it as a cynical response on Shakespeare's part to a royal commission he did not wish to fulfill.[4] Ralph Berry called the play a "brutal farce" and viewed it as a comedy of revenge with decidedly unpleasant overtones, appealing mainly to the audience's sense of superiority over the play's fatuous characters.[5] (It is true that the term "revenge" is used frequently in the dialogue, especially by the two wives as they plot Falstaff's downfall.)

Whatever its shortcomings as literature—its shallow characterizations, carelessness, and inconsistencies— *The Merry Wives of Windsor* never fails to please on the stage. Its vivacity, swift pace, and slapstick foolery have made it a favorite with audiences from the reign of Elizabeth I to that of Elizabeth II. It was quite popular in Shakespeare's time, especially at Court.

In 1702 the inevitable adaptation supplanted the original. Written by John Dennis, it was called *The Comical Gallant; or, The Amours of Sir John Falstaff*. Charles Kean restored the original Shakespeare text in his 1851 production, and American audiences took much pleasure in Augustin Daly's New York production in 1885, which featured John Drew and Ada Rehan.

The comedy has found particular champions among composers. It has been the basis of the libretti of no fewer than nine operas, the most famous of which is Verdi's *Falstaff* (1893), a musical masterpiece that happily transcends its literary source. It may be that music supplies the finishing touch to *The Merry Wives of Windsor*, a comedy that, in spite of its merriment, seems somehow incomplete.

Much Ado about Nothing

The three great comedies of Shakespeare's middle period (roughly 1595 to 1601) are *Much Ado about Nothing, As You Like It*, and *Twelfth Night; or, What You Will.* Written between 1598 and 1600, they are among the best loved and most frequently performed of all Shakespeare's plays. The offhandedness of their titles bespeaks a playwright sure of his craft and creating comedies meant, above all, to please.

The title of *Much Ado about Nothing* suggests that whatever complications and dire events of plot we are asked to suffer through will prove in the end to have been of no consequence, and that is indeed the case with this delightful comedy. Its Italianate intrigues give us a dastardly villain, a wedding aborted by an eleventh-hour renunciation at the altar, a supposed death, and a vow of vengeance. But all ends happily, with the villainy exposed and two couples (once again, the typical Shakespeare love quartet) united in wedlock.

Shakespeare has, as usual, combined multiple story lines into a single coherent plot. At first reading, the principal action seems to be the romance of Claudio and Hero and their victimization by the villainous machinations of Don John the bastard. But in the playing, the Beatrice-Benedick plot emerges as the more entertaining and more believable action, with the antics of Dogberry and the Watch capturing a close second for sheer fun and comic appeal. Indeed, Beatrice, Benedick, and Dogberry are widely recognized as three of the finest acting roles in the Shakespeare canon.

The Claudio-Hero intrigue, which derives from an Italian novella by Matteo Bandello (1480?–1562), presents a number of problems that stretch the reader's credulity, although they seem less troublesome on the stage. (The living presence of actors always minimizes literary inconsistencies.) The chief problem is the characterization of Claudio, who is required by the plot to perform some rather unlikely acts.

Claudio is shown in the first scene of the comedy as a young romantic type and a "right noble" soldier returning from the wars:

> He hath borne himself beyond the promise of his age, doing, in the figure of a lamb, the feats of a lion: he hath indeed better bettered expectation than you must expect of me to tell you how.

Nevertheless, this military "lion" proves unmanly and gullible in readily accepting the false evidence of his beloved Hero's infidelity. Furthermore, not content merely with rejecting her, he allows the marriage plans to proceed so that he may renounce her at the altar, thereby not only humiliating Hero but also bringing public disgrace upon her father Leonato, his host and governor of Messina.

Complicating the character of Claudio even more than his cruel and ungracious behavior in the church is his willingness to accept a substitute bride—a supposed cousin of Hero's—once he is made to believe that Hero has died of grief from his public renunciation of her. These actions are the stuff of Italianate intrigue, and they do not sit well in what is in other respects a fairly realistic comedy.

There are other problems of plotting as well. The entire first act and half of the second are devoted to the development of an intrigue that turns out to be a simple misunderstanding and is then dropped, leading nowhere. Claudio permits the masked Don Pedro, prince of Arragon, to woo Hero in his place but then is misled into believing that the prince has betrayed him and courted Hero for himself. Claudio believes that he has lost his beloved, but this "much ado" is seen to be "about nothing" when Don Pedro tells him (II, i) that Hero is indeed his. Although mistakes and misunderstanding are central themes of the comedy, this incident serves only to delay the more important plot of Don John's villainy, which does not get under way until Act II, scene ii.

Don John's scheme to slander Hero is not altogether convincing, partly because we are never shown the key "window scene" in which the maidservant Margaret impersonates Hero and receives the evil Borachio as a lover. The scene is only narrated to us (III, iii), yet Claudio's renunciation of Hero depends entirely upon the credibility of this unseen event. Then, too, it is never explained how Margaret, a loyal friend to Hero, was made to participate in the deception. Fortunately, Shakespeare was careful to keep Margaret out of the wedding scene (IV, i), for when Claudio accuses Hero, Margaret would necessarily speak up with the truth and the play would end right then and there.

These fairly minor problems in characterization and inconsistency of plot are confined to the Claudio-Hero intrigue. Fortunately they are not serious enough to spoil the comedy, nor do they intrude upon the splendid and thoroughly convincing story of Beatrice and Benedick, the major attractions of *Much Ado about Nothing*.

Shakespeare had sketched the models for Beatrice and Benedick in Rosaline and Berowne (*Love's Labor's Lost*) some five years before, but there was little indication in the earlier couple of the serious emotional involvement that characterizes Beatrice and Benedick. Rosaline and Berowne must part at the end of their comedy, but Beatrice and Benedick are happily united, as we know they will be from the outset.

The convention of a romantic couple pretending indifference and even disdain for each other was to become common in seventeenth-century English comedy, but Shakespeare's treatment of it in *Much Ado about Nothing* was thoroughly innovative. Beatrice and Benedick differ from his earlier pairs of lovers—for example, Bianca and Lucentio, Proteus and Julia, Portia and Bassanio—in their realistic departure from the courtly-love convention with all its attendant poetic indulgences. Significantly, the entire Beatrice-Benedick action is written in straightforward prose, whereas the Claudio-Hero intrigue is in verse. (At one point Beatrice does speak rhymed verse in connection with Benedick, and there it rings conspicuously false— possibly a remnant of an earlier version of the play.)

Beatrice's first line betrays her true concern for Benedick, although she uses the opportunity, typically, to mock him: "I pray you, is Signior Mountanto returned from the wars or no?" (I, i). She goes on to ridicule Benedick's military bravado, attempting to impress the others with her disdain for the man but actually betraying her total preoccupation with him. She can talk of nothing else. Moreover, her uncle

Leonato confirms that her abuse of Benedick is merely part of a long-standing arrangement between the two "adversaries":

> You must not, sir, mistake my niece. There is a kind of merry war betwixt Signior Benedick and her; they never meet but there's a skirmish of wit between them.

When Benedick enters, the two merry warriors engage in a battle of smart repartee, beginning with a volley of insults:

> BEATRICE. I wonder that you will still be talk-
>   ing, Signior Benedick: nobody marks you.
> BENEDICK. What, my dear Lady Disdain! are
>   you yet living?
> BEATRICE. Is it possible disdain should die while
>   she hath such meet food to feed it as Signior
>   Benedick?

Once alone with his friend Claudio and Don Pedro, Benedick protests—perhaps overzealously—that he has only contempt for love, and he proclaims his firm intention never to marry. The other men voice their skepticism (and the audience's), insisting that eventually Benedick will fall victim to Cupid's arrow.

Beatrice has a parallel scene (II, i) with Leonato and his brother Antonio, in which she rejects the idea of marriage and vows to die a maid. Referring to the ancient proverb, "Such as die maids do all lead apes into hell," Leonato asks her if she will be content with that fate, and Beatrice replies:

> No, but [I will go] to the gate; and there will the devil meet me, like an old cuckold, with horns on his head, and say "Get you to heaven, Beatrice, get you to heaven; there's no place

for you maids": so deliver I up my apes, and
away to Saint Peter for the heavens; he shows
me where the bachelors sit, and there live we
as merry as the day is long.

It is the nature of comedy, of course, that such
vehement protestations of disaffection and such vows
of celibacy lead in only one direction—the eventual
coupling of the two protestors. The more they resist
him, the more inevitable is Cupid's victory.

It is Don Pedro who serves as Cupid's emissary in
framing the plan with which "to bring Signior Benedick and the Lady Beatrice into a mountain of affection
the one with the other" (II, i), a plan that results in
two of the comedy's more delightful scenes.

Don Pedro, Claudio, and Leonato stage a conversation (II, iii) before Benedick, who is hiding in the
arbor, during which they talk of Beatrice's secret and
hopeless love for him. Benedick swallows the bait and,
hardly daring to believe what he has heard, vows to be
"horribly in love with her" in return. Hero and
Ursula then stage a similar scene (III, i) for the benefit
of Beatrice, who is hiding in the garden, during which
they discuss Benedick's supposed passion for her.
Beatrice too falls for the ruse, declaring:

> And, Benedick, love on; I will requite thee,
> Taming my wild heart to thy loving hand:
> If thou dost love, my kindness shall incite thee
> To bind our lives up in a holy band.

All that remains at this point is for the two lovers to
confront each other and admit their mutual passion,
putting aside their customary masquerade of mutual
disdain. The way in which Shakespeare brings this
about is a testimony to his particular genius, for the
Beatrice-Benedick confession of love is made to grow
directly out of the quasi-tragic renunciation and pre-

tended death of Hero after the wedding scene. Thus, the love between Beatrice and Benedick, born in scenes of witty raillery and comic trickery, is brought to full maturity in the play's darkest moment, through Beatrice's great need to see her slandered cousin avenged. Benedick becomes her sole champion, and their mutual confession of love culminates in Beatrice's startling but moving injunction to her lover: "Kill Claudio!"—the dramatic high point of the comedy.

Beatrice's plea for vengeance against Claudio puts Benedick's love to the most severe test, for it requires him to challenge his best friend, in effect renouncing their friendship in the name of love. This he does, although fortunately the plot is disentangled before the duel can occur. Although "much ado" again comes to "nothing," the love between Beatrice and Benedick has been put to the test and found durable.

The unraveling of the slander plot is brought about by yet another group of characters—the constable Dogberry, old Verges, and their fellows of the Watch. Although introduced rather late in the play (III, iii), they are important not only as a low-comedy counterpoint to the serious Claudio-Hero plot but also as the audience's guarantee that all will eventually be well. It is the men of the Watch who overhear Conrade and Borachio discussing the dastardly deed that has been perpetrated against Hero's reputation. When they arrest the two villainous connivers and bring them before Dogberry, we are certain that sooner or later Dogberry will, despite his bumbling ineptitude, expose the villainy.

Dogberry is surely one of Shakespeare's finest comic creations. Descended from a line of earlier clowns (Launce, Costard, Bottom, and Launcelot Gobbo), he is at once endearing and exasperating as he bumbles through his constabulary duties, leaving a trail of hilarious malapropisms and absurd pronouncements in his wake.

The plot against Hero would be discovered much earlier were it not for Dogberry's inability to make a clear, direct statement of fact. Appearing before Leonato to expose the villainy (III, iv), he so annoys the Messinian governor with his rambling irrelevancies that Leonato, out of patience, leaves the stage, and the plot against Hero goes unreported. When finally Dogberry brings the guilty Conrade and Borachio before Don Pedro (V, i), his charge against the villains is something less than enlightening:

> Marry, sir, they have committed false report; moreover, they have spoken untruth; secondarily, they are slanders; sixth and lastly, they have belied a lady; thirdly, they have verified unjust things; and, to conclude, they are lying knaves.

The bemused Don Pedro answers him mockingly in kind:

> First, I ask thee what they have done; thirdly, I ask thee what's their offence; sixth and lastly, why they are committed; and, to conclude, what you lay to their charge.

Observing that "this learned constable is too cunning to be understood," Don Pedro turns to Borachio, the accused, who confesses all, finally bringing to light the slander against the innocent Hero. As Borachio tells the prince, speaking of Dogberry and his fellows: "What your wisdoms could not discover, these shallow fools have brought to light."

The slander of Hero is but the pivotal incident in a network of misunderstandings, mishearings, and misreportings that keep *Much Ado about Nothing* in motion. The play depends more than any other Shakespeare comedy upon the transmitting of misinformation. Moreover, while the audience is always fully aware that the information is false, the characters never are. There is no omniscient character—no Oberon or Portia—to share knowledge and awareness with the spectator. The play is a fine example of the skillful employment of dramatic irony; the audience is always superior to the characters in its knowledge of the truth.

It has been suggested that the title of *Much Ado about Nothing* contains a pun that refers to the central device of the comedy's actions. "Nothing" was probably pronounced much like "noting," a word used to mean "overhearing" or "eavesdropping." It is a fitting play on words, for the comedy proceeds through no fewer than eight instances of overhearing, building in importance from the most inconsequential to the most climactic:

1. An unidentified servant of Antonio's overhears the conversation between Claudio and Don Pedro (I, i), in which the latter agrees to court Hero in Claudio's behalf. The servant misinterprets what he has heard and misreports to Antonio that Don Pedro wishes Hero for himself. This misinformation is conveyed also to Leonato (I, ii).

2. Borachio, having eavesdropped on this same Claudio–Don Pedro dialogue, reports it to Don John (I, iii), setting in motion Don John's villainous determination to bring grief to Claudio (for reasons never fully explained).

3. Through a different sort of "noting," Benedick hears Beatrice call him "the prince's jester" and ridicule him unmercifully (II, i), providing ammunition for their "merry war." Both are masked and Benedick assumes that she does not know to whom she is speak-

ing. Thus, he has "overheard" information not intended for his ears—or so he thinks.

4. In this same scene a similar incident of "noting" then occurs. Don John tells the masked Claudio, while pretending to believe that he is Benedick, that Don Pedro intends to marry Hero. Now totally misinformed because of the original eavesdropping and Don John's deception, Claudio, Antonio, and Leonato all believe that Don Pedro wishes to marry Hero. This "ado" comes to "nothing" at Act II, scene i, when Don Pedro reveals the truth.

5. Benedick overhears the conversation between Don Pedro, Claudio, and Leonato (as they intend he should) in which they talk of Beatrice's love for him (II, iii). In this instance, misinformation is reported intentionally, in the spirit of fun.[1]

6. As the complementary incident to number 5, Beatrice is made to overhear Hero and Ursula discuss Benedick's love for her (III, i).

7 and 8. Capping this series of overhearings and misreportings is, confusingly enough, the overhearing of a true report of the overhearing of a false situation (III, iii). The men of the Watch overhear Borachio and Conrade discussing the offstage scene in which Claudio and Don Pedro overhear Borachio make love overtures to Margaret (disguised as Hero), thus impugning Hero's reputation.

A series of "notings" has led from the most inconsequential of misunderstandings to the "much ado" of the plot's climactic incident: Claudio's renunciation of Hero at the altar.

Claudio's cruel treatment of Hero helps to make him one of the least appealing of Shakespeare's romantic young men. He has few admirable qualities, aside from youth and good looks, and his callowness is frequently noted by the other characters. A sampling of words and phrases applied to him throughout the play is revealing: "a young Florentine . . . the figure of a lamb . . . poor hurt fowl . . . boy (repeatedly) . . . Count Comfect, a sweet gallant . . . Lord Lackbeard" and, in attribution, "Boys, apes, braggarts, Jacks, milksops!"

Claudio employs the services of another to do his wooing for him, and his strongest expression of affection for Hero is: "That I love her, I feel" (I, i), He is quick to accept the idea that he has lost Hero to his go-between Don Pedro and goes off in a childish sulk. He is equally quick to believe in her guilt, especially since he has been an eyewitness to her receiving another man at her window (or so he thinks). When he renounces Hero, causing her supposed death, we have little sympathy for the heartless fellow.

It is dramatically necessary that Hero should be presumed dead by most of the play's characters after she swoons before the altar. Her reported death strengthens the bond between Beatrice and Benedick, motivates repentance and atonement in Claudio, and sets the stage for one of the more joyous denouements in Shakespeare. The "resurrection" of a heroine presumed dead provides a powerfully dramatic moment; Shakespeare was to employ the device again in *The Winter's Tale*.

It has been objected that the finale of *Much Ado about Nothing* lacks credibility, partly because of Claudio's ready acceptance of a substitute bride, and partly because of Hero's willingness to wed the man who has brought her such grief. The first objection vanishes if we recall that arranged marriages were the norm in Shakespeare's time. In accepting the "cousin" of Hero as his bride, Claudio pays respect to the family of the girl whose "death" he has brought about, putting honor above self-interest.

The second objection (Hero's willingness to accept Claudio) is of more substance, but Shakespeare's artistry minimizes the difficulty. After unmasking (V, iv), Hero has but one brief speech, and that only incidentally addressed to Claudio:

> CLAUDIO. Another Hero!
> HERO.   Nothing certainer:
>   One Hero died defiled, but I do live,
>   And surely as I live, I am a maid.

Not another word passes between them, and the focus shifts abruptly to the happy union of Beatrice and Benedick, upon which joyful note the comedy ends. The intrigues of their plot quickly disposed of, Claudio and Hero are relegated finally to the background of the picture. So Much Ado about Nothing!

Much Ado about Nothing was evidently fairly popular in Shakespeare's own time but seems largely to have disappeared from the stage during most of the seventeenth century, although bits and pieces of it crop up in various Shakespeare adaptations. It was restored to the stage, more or less intact, by John Rich at the theater in Lincoln's Inn Field in 1721, after which it became one of the more popular of Shakespeare's comedies, due largely to the richness of Beatrice, Benedick, and Dogberry.

The great actor David Garrick had much success as Benedick in a number of productions from 1748 to 1776, playing opposite a variety of Beatrices. Sir Henry Irving and Ellen Terry comprised a successful Beatrice-and-Benedick team, beginning in 1882, and brought their version to America in 1884. Around the turn of the century, the American team of E. H. Sothern and Julia Marlowe earned great success as the two merry warriors, as have a number of English and American actors ever since.

One of the more notable productions of the play in

Joseph Papp's production of *Much Ado about Nothing*, set
circa 1900, for the New York Shakespeare Festival in 1972.
Director: A. J. Antoon; designer, Ming Cho Lee.
GEORGE E. JOSEPH

recent years was that produced by Joseph Papp for
the New York Shakespeare Festival in Central Park
during the summer of 1972. It was so well received
that it was revived on Broadway that fall and played
shortly afterward on national television—all to much
critical acclaim.

Papp's *Much Ado about Nothing* was a perfect example of the successful transference of a Shakespeare
play to an updated setting. It was set in America, circa
1900; its Act I soldiers, including Benedick and Claudio,
were returning presumably from the Spanish-American

War. The play was accompanied throughout by a village park band, and the mise en scène—all lightness and innocent nostalgia—featured such delightful surprises as a vintage automobile, a canoe ride on the lake, and a zany complement of Keystone Kops, led by the indomitable Dogberry (Barnard Hughes). It was a wonderfully effective transposition—one that took full advantage of the fun and minimized the seriousness of this rich comedy.

As You Like It

As You Like It is Shakespeare's chief contribution to pastoralism, a literary mode much in fashion in England during the last two decades of the sixteenth century. Written probably in 1599 or 1600, it observes most of the conventions of the pastoral tradition—escapism, glorification of the bucolic, rustics uttering natural philosophy, and amorous intrigues couched in the language of courtly love.

Shakespeare's source for this comedy was a popular pastoral romance by Thomas Lodge, *Rosalynde: Euphues Golden Legacy* (1590). He followed its story quite closely but made significant additions of his own. Besides changing most of the names in Lodge's tale, he added some new characters—most importantly, Touchstone and Jaques. In so doing, Shakespeare created a comedy that honors the pastoral tradition and at the same time gently spoofs its romantic indulgences.

As You Like It is reminiscent of *A Midsummer Night's Dream* in contrasting the worlds of forest and town, creating in its woodland setting a realm in which the machinery of civilization is temporarily inoperative. But whereas the Athenian wood embodied confusion and error, the Forest of Arden is a setting almost medicinal in its corrective powers—providing succor for the oppressed and religious conversion for the wicked.

The world of the court and its attendant evils are firmly established in the first act of *As You Like It*, leaving the remainder of the comedy free to depict the rustic life in Arden. After Act I, we return briefly to civilization only twice (II, ii, iii; III, i). Thus, the court of Duke Frederick is necessarily depicted with swiftness and economy. Its character is quickly made clear; viciousness predominates.

The "civilized" setting of the court spawns envy, usurpation, injustice, and treachery. In the opening scene Orlando complains that his older brother Oliver mistreats him and has denied him his fair share of their deceased father's estate: "He lets me feed with his hinds, bars me the place of a brother, and . . . mines my gentility with my education." Soon we learn of still more sibling strife; the dukedom has been usurped from its rightful ruler. "The old duke [Duke Senior] is banished by his younger brother the new duke [Frederick]; and three or four loving lords have put themselves into voluntary exile with him, whose lands and revenues enrich the new duke." Misrule is the norm in this environment.

The victims of misrule—chiefly Orlando and Rosalind—exhibit sterling qualities, yet they excite envy rather than admiration in their kin. Oliver plots to have Orlando killed by Charles the wrestler, although he cannot explain even to himself why he is moved to commit such treachery, unless it be simple jealousy:

> My soul, yet I know not why, hates nothing more than he. Yet he's gentle, never schooled and yet learned, full of noble device, of all sorts enchantingly beloved, and indeed so

much in the heart of the world, and especially
of my own people, who best know him, that
I am altogether misprised.

(I, i)

The Frenchman Le Beau warns Rosalind that her
uncle, Duke Frederick the usurper, is about to move
most cruelly against her, even though she has done
no wrong:

> Albeit you have deserved
> High commendation, true applause and love,
> Yet such is now the duke's condition
> That he misconstrues all that you have done.
>
> (I, ii)

Jealousy is, like Oliver's, the Duke's motivation. He
is driven to banish his niece for no other reason "but
that the people praise her for her virtues/And pity her
for her good father's sake" (I, ii). He protests to Celia
that "her [Rosalind's] smoothness,/Her very silence
and her patience/Speak to the people, and they pity
her" (I, iii).

When Orlando foils the wrestling plot by defeating
Charles, Oliver's treachery takes a different course.
He decides to do away with Orlando by setting fire to
his lodging. Adam, the faithful old retainer, warns
Orlando and urges him to flee, but he can attribute the
intended treachery to nothing but Orlando's goodness:

> Know you not, master, to some kind of men
> Their graces serve them but as enemies?
> No more do yours: your virtues, gentle master,
> Are sanctified and holy traitors to you.
> O, what a world is this, when what is comely
> Envenoms him that bears it!
>
> (II, iii)

What a world indeed! The virtuous meet only with injustice.

The world of Arden is, on the other hand, wholly just—a refuge, in fact, for those against whom injustice has been perpetrated. Duke Senior and his "loving lords"; Rosalind, Celia, and Touchstone; Orlando and old Adam—all escape to Arden, disinherited but happier. In Celia's words: "Now go we in content/ To liberty and not to banishment" (I, iii).

We first hear of the forest when Charles the wrestler tells of the old Duke's exile:

> They say he is already in the forest of Arden, and a many merry men with him; and they there live like the old Robin Hood of England: they say many young gentlemen flock to him every day, and fleet the time carelessly, as they did in the golden world.
>
> (I, i)

When we actually arrive in Arden, however, we find that this "golden world" is not untarnished, not without its problems and challenges. Throughout the comedy, in fact, Arden is characterized with ambivalence by all who speak of it. It has its good points and its bad points.

Duke Senior speaks both well and ill of Arden in his opening speech (II, i). Life in the forest is "more sweet than that of painted pomp" and "more free from peril than the envious court" (the court whose envy we have just been witness to). It is a life "exempt from public haunt" and one that "finds tongues in trees, books in the running brooks,/Sermons in stones and good in every thing." Nevertheless, the residents of Arden must cope with "the seasons' difference, as the icy fang/And churlish chiding of the winter's wind" that makes one "shrink with cold." It is a life filled with adversity, even though the "uses of adversity" may be made sweet. Weighing such a life, the Duke concludes: "I would not change it."

Touchstone the fool, a courtier by birth and breeding, also expresses ambivalent attitudes about life in Arden vis-à-vis the courtly life. When he first arrives in the forest, footsore and weary (as are all those newly arrived in Arden), he is something less than enthusiastic: "Ay, now am I in Arden; the more fool I; when I was at home, I was in a better place: but travellers must be content" (II, iv).

In a philosophical dialogue with the old shepherd Corin, Touchstone provides a self-contradictory analysis of the life of an Arden shepherd:

> In respect of itself, it is a good life; but in respect that it is a shepherd's life, it is naught. In respect that it is solitary, I like it very well; but in respect that it is private, it is a very vile life. Now, in respect it is in the fields, it pleaseth me well; but in respect it is not in the court, it is tedious. As it is a spare life, look you, it fits my humour well; but as there is no more plenty in it, it goes much against my stomach.
>
> (III, ii)

The point seems to be that life in Arden is a matter of attitude; goodness is relative. Idyllic pastoralism is subject to interpretation. Corin claims pride in the rustic simplicity of watching "my ewes graze and my lambs suck," but Touchstone sees that as a "simple sin in you, to bring the ewes and the rams together and to offer to get your living by the copulation of cattle" (III, ii).

The melancholy Jaques, who has little good to say of anything, sees life in Arden as a usurpation by men of that which rightly belongs to the beasts. (The First Lord describes Jaques weeping with grief at the sight of a deer that was wounded by a reckless hunter.) In his improvised stanza of lyrics to Amiens's song, "Under the Greenwood Tree" (II, v), Jaques makes it clear that he finds his and his fellows' presence in Arden foolish and perverse:

> If it do come to pass
> That any man turn ass,
> Leaving his wealth and ease,
> A stubborn will to please,
> . . . .
> Here shall he see
> Gross fools as he,
> An if he will come to me.

Whatever its good and bad features, life in Arden is singularly free from the bustling activity and intrigues of life at court. The first act of the comedy includes a fistfight, an attempted murder, a wrestling match, an arson plot, and a banishment. By contrast, the forest life is static. Arden is a relaxing place—a setting for discussion and contemplation. As Orlando points out, "there's no clock in the forest" (III, ii). The inhabitants of Arden are allowed the time to sit and talk.

And talk they do! Duke Senior and his men open the Arden section of the comedy with a discussion of their sylvan life (II, i); later they sing songs and picnic "under the greenwood tree" while Jaques ponders life as theater (II, vii). Corin and Touchstone debate the relative merits of court and country (III, ii). Rosalind and Orlando repeatedly discuss love and courtship (III, ii; IV, i). And Touchstone delivers a satiric discourse on the fine points of quarreling (V, iv). The paucity of overt action and suspenseful intrigue after its first act makes *As You Like It* unique among Shakespeare's comedies.

Like *A Midsummer Night's Dream* and *The Merry Wives of Windsor*, *As You Like It* concludes with a masquelike celebration. The mythical figure of Hymen appears amid "still music" and blesses in verse and song the four happy couples who are to be wed: Orlando and Rosalind, the converted Oliver and Celia, Silvius and Phebe, and Touchstone and Audrey. These eight wedding participants provide a fine sampling of varying motives for the coupling of male and female.

Touchstone has no illusions about his bride-to-be, the slatternly Audrey. He introduces her to the Duke as a "poor virgin, sir, an ill-favoured thing, sir, but mine own" (V, iv). Marriage for Touchstone is a necessity if the desires of the flesh are to be satisfied: "As the ox hath his bow, sir, the horse his curb and the falcon her bells, so man hath his desires; and as pigeons bill, so wedlock would be nibbling" (III, iii). This is love at the level of physical gratification, free from romantic niceties.

At the opposite extreme, of course, is the love between Rosalind and Orlando, possibly the two happiest lovers in all of Shakespeare. Although they conform in the first act to the love-at-first-sight convention, once in Arden they behave unlike any of Shakespeare's other lovers, thanks largely to Rosalind's intelligence and her realistic attitude toward love.

By keeping Rosalind in her male attire and having her persuade Orlando to court "Ganymede" as if "he" were Rosalind, Shakespeare created a delightfully ironic situation—one even more ironic in his own theater, where Rosalind was played by a boy. (What fun it must have been to watch a boy playing the role of a girl who is pretending to be a boy—being wooed by a boy who thinks he is courting a boy pretending to be a girl!) In the course of this relationship, Rosalind has the opportunity to observe Orlando and to be sure of his love for her, while at the same time tempering his idealism and instructing him on the nature of true love.

No other Shakespeare heroine has such an advantage over her beloved.

Orlando is a pleasant but rather ordinary fellow for a Shakespeare lover. He is a good athlete, a poor poet, and—compared to a Berowne or a Benedick—a bit of a dimwit. He behaves at first much like the typical lover in courtly literature—triumphing in combat (the wrestling match) and accepting his lady's token (the chain). He writes love poems and tacks them up on trees, but they are dreadful doggerel—"the very false gallop of verses"—in halting trochaic meter.

Orlando has almost no contact with Rosalind while she is in her own guise. He is in her presence throughout the play but never knows it. Apart from their brief initial encounter, he speaks but one line to her while aware that she is Rosalind—his acceptance of her in the final scene: "If there be truth in sight, you are my Rosalind." For all his appeal as a romantic hero, Orlando is deceived throughout and functions principally as a foil to the character of Rosalind.

Rosalind is one of the more appealing of Shakespeare's young women. She is drawn with considerable complexity—alternately shy and aggressive, vulnerable and self-sufficient, sentimental and sardonic. Her passion for Orlando is genuine, as we see when Celia first tells her that he is in the forest:

> Alas the day! what shall I do with my doublet and hose? What did he when thou sawest him? What said he? How looked he? Wherein went he? What makes he here? Did he ask for me? Where remains he? How parted he with thee? And when shalt thou see him again? Answer me in one word.
>
> (III, ii)

Her passion notwithstanding, she has no illusions about the perils of love, and she rejects the trappings of literary romanticism. She mocks Orlando's love poetry, telling him that "love is merely a madness, and . . . deserves as well a dark house and a whip as madmen do" (III, ii). When Orlando swears that he will die if his Rosalind rejects him, she counters with:

> No, faith, die by attorney. The poor world is almost six thousand years old, and in all this time there was not any man died in his own person, videlicet, in a love-cause. . . . Men have died from time to time and worms have eaten them, but not for love.
>
> (IV, i)

Her rapturous confession to Celia—

> O coz, coz, coz, my pretty little coz, that thou didst know how many fathom deep I am in love! But it cannot be sounded: my affection hath an unknown bottom, like the bay of Portugal.

—is followed almost immediately by her description of Cupid as

> that same wicked bastard of Venus that was begot of thought, conceived of spleen and born of madness, that blind rascally boy that abuses every one's eyes because his own are out.
>
> (IV, i)

That is Rosalind: passionate, changeable, mocking, loving.

Among its many and varied characters, *As You Like It* offers two eccentrics of special interest, Touchstone the fool and the melancholy Jaques. Neither appears in Lodge's *Rosalynde*, the source story. Perhaps Shakespeare felt the need for a dose of cynicism to counteract the saccharine pastoralism of Lodge's tale, for both characters are essentially realists and cynics.

In creating Touchstone, Shakespeare abandoned the line of clowns he had developed earlier (Launce, Bottom, Dogberry), turning instead to a new type of comic figure. Touchstone is the first of the court jesters or "allowed fools" that populate the comedies after 1600; his successors are Feste (*Twelfth Night*), Lavache (*All's Well That Ends Well*), and Trinculo (*The Tempest*).[1]

Unlike the earlier clowns, Touchstone is intelligent, articulate, and deliberately amusing. He never commits malapropisms. He is in all respects a realist—a "touchstone" of true feeling in the midst of the rarefied artifice of pastoralism. He debunks romantic love in his lust for the "foul slut" Audrey and in his reminiscence of an earlier courtship of one Jane Smile: "I remember the kissing of her batlet and the cow's dugs that her pretty chopt hands had milked" (II, iv). He repeatedly ridicules the rustic residents of Arden—Corin, William, Audrey, and Martext the parson—finding little to commend in the pastoral life. Throughout the comedy, Touchstone offers a delightfully earthy counterpoint to the romantic melodies of pastoralism.

Jaques is unique among Shakespeare's characters. His presence in the comedy is indispensable, yet he serves no purpose in advancing the plot. He is always there, but he does nothing. Jaques's character is defined by attitudes, rather than by actions. Duke Senior once briefly illuminates his past, accusing him of having been "a libertine,/As sensual as the brutish sting itself" (II, vii), and we know that he has traveled. But that is all we know. Jaques is cynical, misanthropic, sardonic, and somehow strangely endearing.

In conventional literary terms, Jaques is a "humour," a character dominated by a single trait—in this case, melancholy. He derives from the Elizabethan type of

the malcontent, but Shakespeare went beyond the
stereotype in creating him. His melancholy, which he
thoroughly enjoys ("I do love it better than laughing"),
is unique:

> I have neither the scholar's melancholy, which
> is emulation, nor the musician's, which is
> fantastical, nor the courtier's, which is proud,
> nor the soldier's, which is ambitious, nor
> the lawyer's, which is politic, nor the lady's,
> which is nice, nor the lover's, which is all
> these: but it is a melancholy of mine own,
> compounded of many simples, extracted from
> many objects, and indeed the sundry con-
> templation of my travels, in which my often
> rumination wraps me in a most humourous
> sadness.
>
> (IV, 1)

Like Touchstone, the only character for whom he
expresses any admiration, Jaques counteracts the pastoral mood, thereby setting it in even sharper relief.
In his hilarious dialogue with the lovesick Orlando
(III, ii), he renounces love as the "worst fault" possible. Music to him is a medium for expressing sorrow;
he brags that he can "suck melancholy out of a song,
as a weasel sucks eggs" (II, v). He has but one ambition, by which he would remedy the ills of humankind:

> Give me leave
> To speak my mind, and I will through and
> through
> Cleanse the foul body of the infected world,
> If they will patiently receive my medicine.
>
> (II, vii)

He does then speak his mind, at least in part, in his
great speech beginning "All the world's a stage," one
of the more famous passages in Shakespeare. It cata-

logues the seven ages of man in the most unflattering of images and concludes with a stunning line of monosyllables—the despairing portrait of aged man, "sans teeth, sans eyes, sans taste, sans every thing." Jaques is a true original; Arden would be the less without him.

✱There is much in *As You Like It* to please an audience. In addition to its delightful love intrigues, it offers a fight scene, a wrestling match, a number of songs (more than in any other Shakespeare play), a wedding masque, and a wide and varied range of intriguing characters. It is a comedy true to its title.

Tradition has it that Shakespeare himself played old Adam in the original production of *As You Like It* at the newly built Globe Theatre in 1599. There is no evidence to prove this, however, and no evidence of the comedy's having been acted again during the whole of the seventeenth century. It was not until 1723 that a badly mangled adaptation of the play was revived in London—a version minus Touchstone, Audrey, William, Phebe, and Corin.

Shakespeare's original version (or something close to it) was finally restored to the stage in 1740 at the Drury Lane, and it has become one of the more popular of Shakespeare's comedies in the modern theater. *As You Like It* provided a field day for nineteenth-century scenic designers, who attempted to render Arden in the most elaborate and realistic terms, and it has frequently received outdoor staging, where nature provides the forest setting.

The role of Rosalind has long been a favorite with actresses. Virtually every English actress of note has appeared in the role. Notable American Rosalinds have included Fanny Davenport (ca. 1875), Lily Langtry (1882), Henrietta Crosman (1902), Maude Adams (1910), and Katharine Hepburn (1950, in a record-breaking Broadway run).

A beflowered Touchstone (Alan David) converses with
Jaques (Emrys James) in the 1977 production of *As You
Like It* for the Royal Shakespeare Company. Production
directed by Trevor Nunn; designed by John Napier.
JOHN HAYNES (REPRODUCED BY PERMISSION OF THE GOVERNORS
OF THE ROYAL SHAKESPEARE THEATRE, STRATFORD-UPON-AVON)

A most unusual production of *As You Like It* was staged by the National Theatre Company of Great Britain in 1967. All the roles were played by men, the attempt being (in the words of its director Clifford Williams) to evoke "an atmosphere of spiritual purity which transcends sensuality in the search for poetic sexuality."[2] It was moderately successful and toured America, playing New York in 1974.

The 1977 production of *As You Like It* by the Royal Shakespeare Company employed an unusual visual approach to the comedy, depicting the Forest of Arden in the grip of winter. Stark, abstract, icy tree branches suggested a bleak and hostile environment, and Jaques's melancholy was at least partially explained by a grotesque scar that ran down one side of his face. This writer was put in mind of George Bernard Shaw's comment on Augustin Daly's 1897 production: " 'As You Like It' just as I don't like it."

Twelfth Night; or, What You Will

In his introduction to the New Cambridge edition of *Twelfth Night*, Sir Arthur Quiller-Couch dubbed the play Shakespeare's "Farewell to Comedy." Written probably in 1600 or 1601, this work stands at the summit of the dramatist's career as a writer of happy comedies. After *Twelfth Night*, he was to abandon purely festive comedy in favor of the troubling "dark comedies" and tragicomic romances of his later years.

Although the general tone of *Twelfth Night* is festive, a strain of wistful melancholy runs throughout its principal love plot. If, as has been suggested, the comedy was written especially in observance of Twelfth Night (January 6, the final celebration of the Christmas season), its melancholy is not misplaced, for "Twelfth Night is a feast, and an end to feasting. It implies a sour awareness that the real winter is to come."[1]

This comedy offers a recapitulation of much that Shakespeare had successfully achieved in his earlier comedies. Although it relies on a number of diverse literary sources (at least a dozen), its chief source may be said to be Shakespeare himself. In *Twelfth Night* we find pleasant reminders of *The Comedy of Errors, The Two Gentlemen of Verona, The Merchant of Venice, As You Like It*, and other Shakespeare plays.

The subject of the play is love—not only romantic love (Viola-Orsino-Olivia) but also sibling love (Viola-Sebastian), love of friend (Sebastian-Antonio), carnal love (Sir Toby–Maria), mercenary love (Sir Andrew–Olivia), and self-love (Malvolio). The Duke Orsino launches the love theme in the comedy's opening speech:

> If music be the food of love, play on;
> Give me excess of it, that, surfeiting,
> The appetite may sicken and so die.

Orsino's love for the unapproachable Olivia is self-indulgent and excessive; he is in love with love. He himself admits that his passion is a kind of "fancy," "so full of shapes . . . that it alone is high fantastical" (I, i). Love is, for Orsino, an ideal; he is a courtly lover, and his "fancy" is not rooted in reality. It is significant that Orsino and Olivia never appear on stage together until Act V, scene i (at the height of the confusion over the mistaken identity), where he upbraids her for her supposed marriage to "Caesario." Their courtship is conducted entirely through messages.

Olivia is similarly ruled by fancy, first in her protracted mourning for her brother's death (another manifestation of self-indulgence) and later in her passion for "Caesario," a mere illusion. Olivia wears her grief like a veil of chastity. Her vow to mourn for seven years is wholly fanciful. Like the gentlemen's vow of celibacy in *Love's Labor's Lost*, it is meant to be broken. After Feste, her fool, "dexteriously" proves the folly of her excessive mourning (I, v), her grief easily gives way to yet another form of fancy—her infatuation with Viola, the fictional Caesario.

Because she is enamored of an illusion, Olivia's passion for Viola is expressed in highly conventional language and is not at all realistic. Shakespeare emphasized the artificiality of their "love scenes" together through the use of rhymed couplets (III, i; V, i), conventional courtly-love talk (I, v), and convoluted wordplay:

> OLIVIA. I prithee, tell me what thou think'st of me.
> VIOLA. That you do think you are not what you are.
> OLIVIA. If I think so, I think the same of you.
> VIOLA. Then think you right: I am not what I am.
> OLIVIA. I would you were as I would have you be!
>
> (III, i)

Both Orsino and Olivia, then, are victims of their own fancy, rather than true lovers. It is not surprising, therefore, that both are able, in the final scene, swiftly to switch their affections to more fitting objects. Realizing that the loyal youth he has found so attractive is in reality a girl, Orsino quickly takes Viola for his new "mistress and his fancy's queen." And Olivia has the compliant, solidly male Sebastian to replace the elusive and illusory Caesario.

Although Viola serves as the mediator between these two noble but fancy-ridden lovers, she is no mere go-between. Viola is the comedy's voice of true love, functioning as a corrective for the misdirected affections of both Orsino and Olivia. Her feeling for Orsino is genuine, not mere fancy, and her inability to express it accounts for much of the melancholy of the comedy.

Viola's disguise is, of course, a conventional device in the romantic literature of the time. Shakespeare had employed the convention in creating Julia (*The Two Gentlemen of Verona*), who, like Viola, was forced to serve as proxy for the man she loved and woo her rival; in Portia (*The Merchant of Venice*); and in Rosalind (*As You Like It*). The great difference between Rosalind and Viola, however, is that the former used transvestism to her advantage in winning her love, while Viola's disguise is the chief obstacle to her happiness and the direct cause of her perplexing entanglements. Disguise to Viola is a "wickedness,/Wherein the pregnant enemy does much" (II, ii).

Viola's predicament is quite touching. Unlike Rosalind, she has no confidante; she is a solitary sufferer. Virtually trapped in her disguise, she cannot reveal her love for her master until he is purged of his passion for Olivia. She can only watch and wait, at the same time pleading his hopeless case before the countess. Her scenes with the Duke are underscored by melancholy music ("Come away, come away, death" in II, iv) and focused on talk of love's sorrows—unrequited passion, inconstancy, fleeting youth, and so on. She can declare her love to the Duke only through veiled allusions:

> My father had a daughter loved a man,
> As it might be, perhaps, were I a woman,
> I should your lordship.
> . . . .
> She never told her love,
> But let concealment, like a worm i' the bud,
> Feed on her damask cheek: she pined in
> thought,
> And with a green and yellow melancholy
> She sat like patience on a monument,
> Smiling at grief. Was not this love indeed?
>
> (II, iv)

Viola is supremely feminine, despite her masculine attire. She affects none of the blustering bravado and masculinity that characterize Rosalind. When forced to the point of duelling with Sir Andrew, she is tempted to unmask rather than fight: "I am one that had rather go with sir priest than sir knight" (III, iv). Her femininity is readily acknowledged by Orsino:

> For they shall yet belie thy happy years,
> That say thou art a man: Diana's lip
> Is not more smooth and rubious; thy small pipe
> Is as the maiden's organ, shrill and sound,
> And all is semblative a woman's part.
>
> (I, iv)

The happy conclusion to Viola's predicament is twofold. She gains not only the lover she has so loyally and ardently served but also the brother she had believed lost. Fearing at first that her twin Sebastian has been drowned in the shipwreck (an echo from *The Comedy of Errors*), she later finds reason to believe that he, too, may have survived the calamity. When she is reviled by Antonio, who believes her to be her twin, she soliloquizes:

> Prove true, imagination, O, prove true,
> That I, dear brother, be now ta'en for you!
> . . . .
> He [Antonio] named Sebastian: I my brother
>   know
> Yet living in my glass; even such and so
> In favour was my brother, and he went
> Still in this fashion, colour, ornament,
> For him I imitate: O, if it prove,
> Tempests are kind and salt waves fresh in love.
>
> (III, iv)

This scene does much to relieve the audience's anxiety over Viola's fate; we feel that eventually brother and sister will be reunited and that Viola's true identity will then be revealed. When the moment comes (V, i), it provides one of the more moving scenes in the comedy. The love between Viola and Sebastian, who stand side by side in life, puts into sharp relief the fruitless love of Olivia for her dead brother's memory. As always in Shakespeare's happy comedies, the force of life prevails.

The role of Antonio the sea captain is a small one, but it allows Shakespeare once again to affirm the sanctity of male friendship, through Antonio's devotion to Sebastian. Antonio entrusts his purse to his friend and later mistakenly attempts to claim it from "Caesario," an incident found also in *The Comedy of Errors*. But here the confusion of identities achieves an effect more serious than that of mere farcical mixup. Antonio's deep hurt over his friend's supposed denial and betrayal of him, together with Viola's bewilderment at the stranger's accusations, is truly affecting— one of those poignant touches that take this comedy to a level deeper than that of pure fun.

The amity between Antonio and Sebastian recalls earlier friendships in Shakespeare's comedies: Proteus and Valentine (*The Two Gentlemen of Verona*), Antonio and Bassanio (*The Merchant of Venice*), and Benedick and Claudio (*Much Ado about Nothing*), to name but a few. The version here, however, is dramatically stronger in that it stands in contrast to weaker manifestations of love—the fancy-mongering of Orsino's romantic melancholy, Malvolio's narcissism, and so on. It is struck from the true metal that shines out in the best of Shakespeare's portrayals of love, whether platonic or sexual.

Whatever the underlying wistfulness of its principal action, *Twelfth Night* provides unalloyed fun through a subplot that presents a fairly realistic portrait of life in an English manor house in Shakespeare's time, its

Illyrian setting notwithstanding. Olivia's household, with its puritanical steward, wastrel knights, waiting ladies, and resident jester, seems somehow more appropriate to the town of *The Merry Wives of Windsor* than to the fanciful land of Illyria. Its characters, at any rate, are decidedly English.

This broadly comic subplot, peopled by Sir Toby Belch, Sir Andrew Aguecheek, Maria, Fabian, and Malvolio, probably represents a conscious effort on Shakespeare's part to capitalize on the popularity of "humours" comedy, a comic mode that was successful in the English theater around 1600.

Developed principally by Ben Jonson, the comedy of humours utilized type characters in satirizing contemporary behavior. Humours characters are motivated by a single, dominant trait or passion that determines their behavior in any given situation. Traditionally, their names indicate their humours, as is the case with our comedy's three leading figures of fun: Sir Toby Belch, Sir Andrew Aguecheek, and Malvolio.

Sir Toby and Sir Andrew are surely the most delightful comedy team in Shakespeare—a sort of Elizabethan Laurel and Hardy. Sir Toby Belch (an appropriate name for a gluttonous, drunken merrymaker) is Sir John Falstaff in miniature; his sole mission in the comedy is to revel, cause mischief, and gull Sir Andrew out of as much money as possible. Their relationship is typical of those in Jonsonian comedy, where trickery and gulling are common fare.

Sir Andrew Aguecheek (a name suggesting a wasted or sickly countenance) is the most fatuous simpleton since Slender (*The Merry Wives of Windsor*), whom he surpasses in comic appeal. Little more than Sir Toby's puppet, Aguecheek allows himself to be totally manipulated by the fat knight, who cheats him of his money under the pretense of aiding his suit to Olivia— a hopeless cause to begin with. He admits his foolishness—"Methinks sometimes I have no more wit than a Christian or an ordinary man has" (I, iii)—and acknowledges that "many do call me fool" (II, v). Beside Sir Toby he cuts a ludicrous figure—thin, pale, with straight yellow hair that "hangs like flax on a distaff"—and he reaps for his loyalty to the fat knight only a broken head and a dressing down.

The fun of gulling reaches its peak in the letter plot —the trick played by the knights, Fabian, and Maria on Malvolio, Olivia's household steward. Malvolio ("ill-will") is unique among Shakespeare's creations. No figure in the earlier comedies foreshadows this austere, self-centered, churlish, puritanical, social-climbing killjoy. He is possibly the most satiric of all Shakespeare's comic characters; we can detect almost no sympathy for him on the part of his creator. He is given no redeeming features, except that of making us laugh. Even then, our laughter is occasioned not by any innately amusing qualities (wittiness, good humor, ingenuousness) but by our contempt for his pretentiousness. We can feel some affection for the hedonistic Sir Toby and the bumbling Sir Andrew, for they at least seem partially aware of their follies. Malvolio deceives even himself in affecting his haughty demeanor. He finds no fault or flaw in his looking glass. In this respect he is the most Jonsonian character in the comedy—the most thoroughly "humourous."

We first see Malvolio putting down Olivia's fool with sneering contempt, generally spoiling everyone's fun. Olivia tags him immediately: "O, you are sick of self-love, Malvolio, and taste with a distempered appetite" (I, v). When he breaks up the late-night drinking party of the fool and the merry knights, Maria calls him

> a time-pleaser; an affectioned ass, that cons state without book and utters it by great

swarths: the best persuaded of himself, so crammed, as he thinks, with excellencies, that it is his grounds of faith that all that look on him love him.

(II, iii)

Malvolio's humour of self-love leads to his bold ambition to marry his mistress, the Countess Olivia. To an Elizabethan audience this represented an unpardonable affront to the social order—an offense that fully deserved punishment. His pretensions toward Olivia have nothing to do with love; she is simply the instrument through which he hopes to jump class and become "Count Malvolio." This, coupled with his put-down of the fool and his disruption of the party fun, sets him up as an apt target for comic revenge.

The revenge is sweet, especially for the audience. Persuaded by the supposed love letter from Olivia (dropped in his way by the scheming Maria), he obeys its commands and appears before his mistress in yellow stockings ("a colour she abhors"), cross-gartered ("a fashion she detests"), smiling like an idiot and kissing his hand—a perfectly ludicrous figure. Olivia, thinking him mad, has him confined.

It has sometimes been objected that Malvolio's treatment is excessively harsh: locked in a dark room as a madman and tormented by the fool. But considering the gravity of his offense (and the fact that the Elizabethans considered the torment of the insane to be great sport) Shakespeare's audience would not have found it so. Malvolio's final exit in high dudgeon ("I'll be revenged on the whole pack of you") should be played as comic, not movingly pathetic, as was frequently the case by late-nineteenth-century actors. Malvolio was, is, and ever should be an "affectioned ass" who gets his comeuppance. The gulling of Malvolio is the comic highlight of *Twelfth Night.*

There yet remains one major character in *Twelfth Night* deserving of attention: Feste, Olivia's fool. He is the finest of Shakespeare's comic fools. Although of the same character type as Touchstone (*As You Like It*), he is more consistently drawn and more entertaining. He is also more innocent; Feste's wit is fit for children's ears. (*Twelfth Night* is, incidentally, Shakespeare's "cleanest" comedy.)

Aside from Viola, Feste is the only character to commute between Olivia's house and the court of Orsino. And like Viola, he functions as a moderating and corrective influence in the action, principally in the capacity of commentator or *raisonneur*. He is only tangentially involved in any of the play's intrigues and functions largely outside the action. (Although he is present when Maria contrives the false-letter device, he is strangely absent during its execution, having been replaced by the nondescript newcomer Fabian.)

Feste is the most philosophical and objective of Shakespeare's fools. He is paradoxically wise in his folly, whereas the other characters are foolish in their supposed wisdom. His stock-in-trade is language; he styles himself Olivia's "corrupter of words." Being an "allowed fool" or professional wit, he can use words with impunity to make telling observations on the other characters. For example, in a clever bit of convoluted reasoning (I, v) he points out to his mistress that she is a fool to mourn her brother's death. Again, after singing at Orsino's court (II, iv) he chides the Duke (albeit in veiled terms) for inconstancy and excessive melancholy. Feste is a chorus character who keeps the truth before us.

Viola has but one brief encounter with the fool, during which she, too, is victimized by his incisive wit and wheedled into paying for his foolery (III, i). Nevertheless, she admires his professional skill and nicely sums up his abilities:

> This fellow is wise enough to play the fool;
> And to do that well craves a kind of wit:
> He must observe their mood on whom he jests,
> The quality of persons, and the time,
> And, like the haggard, check at every feather
> That comes before his eye. This is a practice
> As full of labour as a wise man's art:
> For folly that he wisely shows is fit;
> But wise men, folly-fall'n, quite taint their wit.

Feste serves as Master of Revels for this Twelfth Night comedy. His name, suggestive of festivity, speaks for the play as a whole. His spirit, wit, and intellect do much to temper the sentiment of the comedy's romantic entanglements and to heighten its comic tone. Feste sings the three songs in *Twelfth Night* and brings the play to a close, alone on the stage, with a musical promise to its audience:

> A great while ago the world begun,
>   With hey, ho, the wind and the rain,
> But that's all one, our play is done,
>   And we'll strive to please you every day.

Twelfth Night is an exceptionally stageworthy comedy, thanks mainly to the appealing roles of Malvolio and Viola. Many actors and actresses, both English and American, have earned success in these roles. One early Malvolio of note was Charles Macklin, whose Drury Lane production in 1741 served to restore the comedy's popularity after it had been neglected for more than a hundred years. (Although *Twelfth Night* was popular in its own time, it was infrequently performed after the Restoration.) Tragic actors like John Philip Kemble and Sir Henry Irving were drawn to Malvolio and are credited with emphasizing his serious side and robbing the "affectioned ass" of much of his fun.

Sir Andrew Aguecheek (Peter Silbert), Feste (Jeff Brooks), and Sir Toby Belch (Richard Riehle) carouse drunkenly in Act II, Scene iii, of *Twelfth Night*, in the 1974 production at the Oregon Shakespearean Festival (Ashland). Production directed by Jim Edmondson; costumes by John David Ridge; setting by Richard L. Hay.
HANK KRANZLER

The success of any production of *Twelfth Night* invariably rests with its Viola. Several American actresses have earned acclaim in the role: Julia Marlowe (1890), Jane Cowl (1930), Helen Hayes (1940), Beatrice Straight (1941), and Katharine Hepburn (1960), to name but a few.

Like *The Two Gentlemen of Verona*, a comedy

with which it bears some kinship, *Twelfth Night* appeared recently in a rock-musical adaptation. *Your Own Thing* opened in New York in 1968 and subsequently achieved considerable success on its national tours. This exuberant and affectionate spoof of Shakespeare's comedy was set in "Manhattan Island, Illyria," and utilized some of Shakespeare's dialogue, along with contemporary slang and rock songs. Orson (Orsino) was a theatrical agent and Olivia operated a discotheque (!). Like the musical *Two Gentlemen of Verona*, *Your Own Thing* serves as evidence of the universal appeal of Shakespeare's comic mode.

Troilus and Cressida

Some readers might be surprised to find *Troilus and Cressida* included in a discussion of Shakespeare's comedies, for there is precious little about the play that is conducive to laughter—unless it be laughter spawned by mockery and contempt. If we are to consider it a comedy at all, we must view it as one quite different from the ten merry and brightly colored works that culminated in the festive *Twelfth Night*. *Troilus and Cressida* is painted in the dark tones that characterize all seven of Shakespeare's final comedies, excepting possibly *The Tempest*.

There is a history of confusion over the appropriate classification of *Troilus and Cressida*. Its first printing, the quarto of 1609, includes a preface suggesting that this is one of Shakespeare's wittiest comedies. In the First Folio (1623), however, the play is grouped with the tragedies as "The Tragedie of Troylus and Cressida." Some modern critics still find tragic implications in the play. The Hardin Craig edition of Shakespeare includes it among the tragedies, and E. K. Chambers, in 1940, called it a "tragedy of disillusionment."[1]

Nevertheless, the general practice in modern criticism is to group *Troilus and Cressida* with *All's Well That Ends Well* and *Measure for Measure* as three "dark comedies," "bitter comedies," or "problem comedies." Oscar J. Campbell called the play a "comical satire" and saw it as Shakespeare's conscious imitation of the style of Ben Jonson and John Marston.[2] The New Cambridge editor, Alice Walker, agreed with this Jonsonian identification, claiming that the play aims at the "correction of manners through the ridicule of folly."[3] Such diversity of viewpoints proves simply that *Troilus and Cressida* cannot be readily classified. It is unique among Shakespeare's plays.

Shakespeare relied upon two principal sources for this work, both of which were familiar to his contemporaries. For the background of the Trojan War and all the figures associated with it, he drew upon Homer's *Iliad*. The story of Troilus and the faithless Cressida was a medieval tale of considerable popularity, probably most effectively told in Chaucer's late-fourteenth-century treatment of it, *Troilus and Criseyde*.

Shakespeare's treatment of both sources, and especially his characterizations, are distinctly his own. Homer's monumental heroes of Greece and Troy are reduced to luxurious, self-serving, and prideful fools, and the affair between the title characters is drawn as a seamy coupling of lustful sensualists, urged on by Pandarus, chief pimp and whoremonger. As the American stage director Joseph Papp observed:

> In *Troilus and Cressida* it is almost possible to dislike every character in the play, for in it we find that we can choose from the most despicable assortment of lowlife ever crammed together in a single work: panders, traitors,

connivers, whores, cuckolds, seducers, rapists, lechers, murderers, liars, fornicators, and adulterers.[4]

Troilus and Cressida is certainly the most unpleasant of all Shakespeare's plays. Its characters behave in ways that do little to affirm the finer facets of human nature, and its language is the most coarse and obscene in Shakespeare. Much of this is due to the characters and speeches of Thersites and Pandarus—the former specializing in scurrilous invective and the latter in frank images of sexual luxury.

Both Thersites and Pandarus serve as chorus figures who comment upon the play's characters and action. But whereas Pandarus is integral to the movement of the plot—bringing Troilus and Cressida together and superintending their coupling—Thersites has no function in the plot, aside from commentary.

Thersites appears as a character in the *Iliad*, but Shakespeare turned him into the Elizabethan type of the political malcontent—bitter, disillusioned, and always ready to impute the foulest of motives to all human actions. He can also be seen as a sort of perversion of the "allowed fool" character that Shakespeare had so merrily managed in *As You Like It* and *Twelfth Night*. Thersites is a Feste gone foul. Rather than wit, he gives us raillery, often unfounded and generalized. There is not a civil word from his lips, and in the course of his scurrilous outbreaks he smears and befouls every major character: Nestor, Ulysses, Ajax, Achilles, Patroclus, Helen, Paris, Menelaus, Troilus, and Cressida. Thersites almost single-handedly establishes the unsavory tone of this play.

There are three principal focal points in the play's action, none of which is handled with Shakespeare's customary artistry. The chief intrigue is the affair between Troilus and Cressida, abetted by her uncle

Pandarus. Second, and perhaps equally important, is the practice of Ulysses (the only character in the play who behaves with any degree of wisdom) on the proud Achilles, who luxuriates in his tent with Patroclus, his "masculine whore," and refuses to do battle against the Trojans. Third is the enmity and confrontation between Hector and Achilles, in which the latter ignominiously has his Myrmidons ambush the unarmed Trojan and claims the victory for himself.

Encompassing all three of these plot lines and serving as background to both the war and the play's action is the rape of Helen by Paris and the issue of whether the Trojans will return her to the Greeks. Helen appears only briefly (III, i) and is seen to be a simpering housewife, in ironic contrast to the heroic terms with which the Trojans speak of her. Despite the briefness of her appearance, however, her influence is felt throughout the play. It is the issue of Helen—her abduction and her fate—that serves to fuse the sexual and military themes within the total drama.

The Troilus-Pandarus-Cressida plot is subject to varying interpretations and suffers from flaws in dramatic construction. This is no Romeo-and-Juliet love affair. The frank sexuality of their involvement, stage-managed by the leering bawd Pandarus, robs their intrigue of any romance.

What are we to make of Troilus? Is he an ardent lover in the Romeo tradition or merely a young lecher who, having successfully gotten into Cressida's bed, is just as happy to be rid of her? His rhetoric at the prospect of coupling with Cressida is so extravagant as to seem almost a parody of Shakespearean love talk:

> No, Pandarus: I stalk about her door,
> Like a strange soul upon the Stygian banks
> Staying for waftage. O, be thou my Charon,

And give me swift transportation to those fields
Where I may wallow in the lily-beds
Proposed for the deserver!

(III, ii)

One can hardly resist comparing the "morning
after" scene between Troilus and Cressida with that
between Romeo and Juliet. The Veronese lovers awoke
to the trilling of larks, regretting the approach of
"jocund day," which stood "tiptoe on the misty
mountain tops," and swore their willingness to die for
each other. Troilus comes out of Cressida's bedroom
complaining of the cold, hearing "ribald crows," and
cursing the brevity of the night:

> Beshrew the witch! with venomous wights she
>> stays
> As tediously as hell, but flies the grasps of love
> With wings more momentary-swift than
>> thought.

(IV, ii)

He appears not to have had his fill. He insists that
Cressida go back to bed, for fear she will catch cold
and *blame him!* Pandarus then enters with smirky
jokes about lost maidenheads and a sleepless night. It
is all quite sordid.

When Troilus learns from Aeneas a few lines later
that Cressida is to be surrendered to the Greeks in
exchange for Antenor, his reaction is most telling:

> TROILUS.   Is it so concluded?
> AENEAS. By Priam and the general state of
>> Troy:
> They are at hand and ready to effect it.
> TROILUS. How my achievements mock me!
> I will go meet them: and, my Lord Aeneas,
> We met by chance; you did not find me
>> here.

No outrage, no grief, no resistance! "Is it so con-cluded?" The loss of Cressida will "mock" his "achievements"—a blow to his pride. And what is worse, he is ashamed to have been found at Cressida's house. Troilus is hardly a model lover.

The Troilus-Cressida action presents structural prob-lems as well. We first see Cressida in an extended scene with Pandarus (I, ii), in which she disparages Troilus and engages in some coarse, prosaic banter with her uncle. Our general impression is of a wise-cracking tart who has no interest in Troilus. It is only after this scene that she soliloquizes her true feelings and we learn that she is as hungry for the Trojan as he is for her. The potential irony in her pretended in-difference to Troilus is unrealized, because we did not know she was pretending. The entire Cressida-Pan-darus scene is, dramatically, not only wasted but misleading.

What should, moreover, be a key scene in Pan-darus's campaign to win his niece's favors for Troilus is absent from the play. At the end of Act I, scene ii, Cressida has left Pandarus with the firm avowal that she will have nothing to do with Troilus. We never see her again until Act III, scene ii, when, inexplicably, Pandarus brings Troilus to her for what is obviously a prearranged assignation. We are neither shown nor told how all this came about. In fact, Cressida has been absent from the stage for so long a time that the audience does well even to remember her.

Finally, Cressida becomes a faithless woman and gives herself to Diomedes. The legend dictates that she must. But her abrupt descent into perfidy is unprepared and unmotivated. In all her dealings with Troilus we find no hint that she is a woman capable of breaking her vow of faithfulness. Indeed, up to this point she has been the more credibly constant of the two. Yet she abruptly changes character once she enters the

Greek camp, lasciviously bestowing kisses on all the Greeks and causing Ulysses to comment:

> Fie, fie upon her!
> There's language in her eye, her cheek, her lip,
> Nay, her foot speaks; her wanton spirits look
>   out
> At every joint and motive of her body.
>
> (IV, v)

This wanton is not the same Cressida we last saw, protesting her fidelity in the face of Troilus's doubts. She is the Cressida of the legend, but she is not credible as a dramatic character.

The Achilles action is similarly marred by poor plotting and obscurity. Achilles' motivation for languishing in his tent is never entirely clear. At first we are told by Ulysses that pride is Achilles' flaw:

> The great Achilles, whom opinion crowns
> The sinew and the forehead of our host,
> Having his ear full of his airy fame,
> Grows dainty of his worth and in his tent
> Lies mocking our designs.
>
> (I, iii)

The other Greeks confirm this diagnosis, and Ulysses then frames an elaborate "practice" to cure Achilles of his pride. In a rigged lottery, Ajax is to be chosen to meet the Trojan Hector in combat, thus piquing Achilles. This plot fails to have any effect on Achilles, however, and serves mainly to puff up the dull-witted Ajax.

Then, in Act III, an entirely new motivation for Achilles' refusal to fight is introduced. Ulysses accuses him of being in love with one of the daughters of old Priam, the Trojan king. Achilles himself later admits that this is his reason for wanting to avoid battle with Hector, who is the brother of his beloved Polyxena:

> My sweet Patroclus, I am thwarted quite
> From my great purpose in to-morrow's battle.
> Here is a letter from Queen Hecuba,
> A token from her daughter, my fair love,
> Both taxing me and gaging me to keep
> An oath that I have sworn. I will not break it:
> Fall Greeks; fail fame; honour or go or stay;
> My major vow lies here, this I'll obey.
>
> (V, i)

If Achilles' vow to Polyxena is indeed the reason for his refusal to fight, this knowledge comes to us unreasonably late in the play, and the entire practice of Ulysses on Achilles' pride, via the lottery, is rendered pointless. And as an additional complication, it is suggested in at least two places that Achilles is kept from battle by the influence of his "sweet Patroclus" upon him. Thersites strongly suggests a sexual relationship between the two (V, i), and Patroclus himself tells Achilles that the other Greeks "think my little stomach to the war/And your great love to me restrains you thus" (III, iii). In all, the entire business of Achilles' motivations is botched.

The ending of *Troilus and Cressida* is unsatisfactory. Hector emerges briefly in the fifth act as a quasi-tragic figure, but his murder is more pathetic than genuinely moving. The several brief battle scenes are dramatically confusing, and apart from Hector's rather pointless death, nothing is truly concluded. Both Troilus and Cressida live on—he presumably as a bitter and disillusioned soldier and she as Diomedes' whore. The Trojan War goes on, Hector having been slain and Achilles proved an ignominious murderer. Finally, Pandarus the pimp delivers an epilogue in which he bequeaths to the audience his venereal diseases. *Troilus and Cressida* is a strange play indeed.

Cressida's groom (Clive Swift, left), Pandarus (Paul Rogers) and Cressida (Rosemary Harris) in a scene from Tyrone Guthrie's 1956 version of *Troilus and Cressida* for London's Old Vic.

It is also one of the least frequently performed of all Shakespeare's plays. It was probably not acted in Shakespeare's lifetime—not in the public theaters, at any rate. A very free adaptation of the play, written by John Dryden in 1679, was performed occasionally throughout the Restoration years and the eighteenth century, but Shakespeare's original text had to wait until 1907 for its first recorded production. It was produced in London by Charles Fry, with little success.

In 1912, William Poel's Elizabethan Stage Society mounted *Troilus and Cressida* on an Elizabethan-style stage, with Renaissance costuming. Making her professional debut as Cressida in that production was Edith Evans, later to become one of England's greatest actresses. The Cassandra was Hermione Gingold. The first recorded American production of the play was in 1916 at Yale University.

More recent productions of note have included Tyrone Guthrie's 1956 Old Vic staging in nineteenth-century dress, and the Stratford, Connecticut, production in 1961, costumed in the American Civil War period.

The chief difficulties in presenting *Troilus and Cressida* on the stage lie in its confusing and episodic structure and in its long, rhetorical speeches, especially those in Acts I and III. Nevertheless, it can be made to work in the theater, with intelligent staging and sufficient visual appeal. A 1972 version at the Oregon Shakespeare Festival in Ashland served to persuade this writer that *Troilus and Cressida*, despite its flaws, can be made stageworthy.

All's Well That Ends Well

All's Well That Ends Well, a dark comedy, has never been popular with audiences, and the critical consensus is that it is one of Shakespeare's least successful plays. G. B. Harrison, in his edition of Shakespeare, dismissed it as an " 'interlude,' a means of passing away a couple of hours with a play that never demands too much emotion or thought." Sir Arthur Quiller-Couch, editor of the New Cambridge edition, held the play to be "one of Shakespeare's worst," and H. B. Charlton spoke (perhaps with tongue in cheek) of the work as illustrating a "nymphomaniac succeeding in her quest and the whole worthless loveless bargain sanctified by the name of marriage."[1]

The principal problem with this problem comedy, as with *Troilus and Cressida*, is its ambiguity and the resulting uncertainty with which we must assess its characters—especially Helena and Bertram. This ambiguity affects also the moral implications of the comedy, the ethical values of which are tenuous and shifting. Some of this moral ambiguity can be attributed to Shakespeare's source: the ninth tale of the third day from Boccaccio's *Decameron*. He followed this tale fairly closely in composing the Bertram-Helena intrigue. (The characters of the Countess, Lafeu, and the clown Lavache, as well as the comic subplot of Parolles's unmasking, are Shakespeare's original inventions and, significantly enough, the most successful elements of the comedy.)

The modern reader is perhaps less able to accept the moral tone of the Boccaccio source tale than was Shakespeare's original audience. The "bed trick" (used also in *Measure for Measure*), by which Helena tricks Bertram into sleeping with her, grates upon modern sensibilities. Helena herself can be interpreted as inordinately self-serving and deceitful—first in forcing herself upon a man who obviously can't abide her, then in pursuing him and playing upon his lust for another woman in order to get herself pregnant by him. Add to this unpleasantness a "hero" (Bertram) who is possibly the most self-centered, dishonorable cad in all of Shakespeare, and the problems of the comedy become obvious.

Notwithstanding the modern reader's possible objections to Helena's behavior, Shakespeare probably intended his audience to view her as wholly noble and fully justified in pursuing Bertram and perpetrating the bed trick. To an Elizabethan she would appear clever and virtuous. Arranged marriages were, after all, somewhat the norm, and her claim to Bertram's bed was irrefutable, whether he liked it or not. Aside from these ethical questions, however, there is considerable difficulty in the way Helena is presented dramatically. Her motives and intentions are never made entirely clear.

We know for certain that Helena loves Bertram, as she tells us so in the first scene and readily confesses it to the Countess (I, iii). But she makes no explicit statement of her intention to use the curing of the

King's fistula as a device for ensnaring the boy. Her true intentions become clear only in retrospect, after Act II, scene iii. Similarly, her design in following Bertram to Florence is never stated. If we take her speeches at face value, we can only conclude that she is resigned to losing her husband and going off to become Saint Jaques' pilgrim (see III, ii, and III, iv). Yet in Act III, scene v, she unexplainably appears in Florence and lays the plot to substitute herself in Diana's bed for the assignation with Bertram. Moreover, her reputed death, abruptly announced in Act IV, scene iii, comes as a complete surprise to us as well as to the other characters. There is throughout a singular lack of dramatic preparation for Helena's designs and actions.

The character of Bertram offers even more serious problems. It is almost impossible not to consider him a thorough cad, unworthy of Helena. Indeed, Shakespeare seems to have gone to deliberate pains to alter Boccaccio's original (Beltramo) and make him, according to W. W. Lawrence, a "thoroughly disagreeable, peevish, and vicious person."[2]

In the course of the comedy Bertram abandons his wife, disobeys the King, runs away to Florence with his foppish companion Parolles, commits adultery by seducing a virgin (or so he thinks), and finally lies to all in a desperate attempt to extricate himself from the entanglements he alone has caused. Dr. Samuel Johnson summarized Bertram as

> a man noble without generosity, and young without truth; who marries Helen as a coward, and leaves her as a profligate: when she is dead by his unkindness, sneaks home to a second marriage, is accused by a woman whom he has wronged, defends himself by falsehood, and is dismissed to happiness.[3]

There are, of course, dramatic elements that tend to mitigate Bertram's viciousness and arouse in us some sympathy for him. His youth and callowness are stressed constantly by the older characters. The Countess gives the clear impression that she considers her son an "unseason'd courtier" whose "blood and virtue/Contend for empire" in him (I, i). Lafeu refers to him as an "unbaked and doughy youth" (IV, v), and the King chastises the "proud scornful boy" for his "youth and ignorance" (II, iii). Bertram is also somewhat ennobled in our eyes by the simple fact that the virtuous Helena is so determined to have him. He gains worth, as it were, by reflection. But most importantly, we are told repeatedly that Bertram is misled by the corrupting influence of the worthless Parolles, who is, according to the Countess,

> A very tainted fellow, and full of wickedness.
> My son corrupts a well-derived nature
> With his inducement.
>
> (III, ii)

In establishing this "corruption" Shakespeare pulled off a bit of dramatic legerdemain, for although we are constantly reminded by the other characters that Parolles is a bad influence, we never see the corruption at work. He certainly has nothing to do with Bertram's dislike for Helena or his abandoning her. At most, Parolles simply approves of Bertram's intention to take flight.

Parolles himself is, aside from the weak-witted clown Lavache, the only comical character in the play. And he is an important one. The subplot of his torment and unmasking, although but weakly related to the main plot, occupies a significant portion of the action. Parolles appears in thirteen of the play's twenty-three scenes. His unmasking (IV, iii) is the longest scene in the comedy and stands at its structural center. The unmasking of Parolles substitutes for the critical scene of the Bertram-Helena plot, for we cannot, of course, witness the bed trick in actual performance.

As a character, Parolles ("words") probably satirizes a type of foppish soldier-of-fortune well known in Shakespeare's London. His boasting and military bravado relate him to the classical comic type of the miles gloriosus, but his relationship to Bertram suggests the type of the parasite. His supposed corruption of the young count might be viewed as a watered-down version of Sir John Falstaff's relationship with Prince Hal in *1 Henry IV*.

We know of Parolles to a great extent by what the other characters say of him, rather than by what we see him do. Helena first introduces him as a "notorious liar" and Mariana later calls him a "filthy officer." Lafeu openly ridicules him, and the French Lord describes him to Bertram as a "most notable coward, an infinite and endless liar, an hourly promise-breaker, the owner of no one good quality worthy your lordship's entertainment" (III, vi). Parolles' outlandish dress serves as the outward display of his inner vacuity. He affects "scarfs and bannerets"; Diana calls him a "jack-an-apes with scarfs." "The soul of this man is in his clothes," says Lafeu (II, v).

When acted by a skillful comedian, the part of Parolles can be comical and entertaining, but the character is not very skillfully drawn and his relationship to the main action is tenuous at best. Quiller-Couch conceived Parolles to be "on the whole, with all his concern in this play, about the inanest of all Shakespeare's inventions," and H. B. Charlton referred to him as "that shapeless lump of cloacine excrement."[4]

Nevertheless, were it not for the boastful, cowardly, foppish Parolles—his ridicule and exposure—we would enjoy precious little laughter in this comedy. Although we find a clown (Lavache) among the dramatis personae, he is a poor example of the type and has little to do with the plot. Quiller-Couch saw him as a "poor thin fellow" of no consequence, asserting that "Shakespeare could have made him ten times a better Clown than he is." The Countess is on the mark when she calls him a "foul-mouthed and calumnious knave" (I, iii). Compared to Feste and Touchstone, Lavache is a dimwit.

More than any of Shakespeare's earlier comedies, *All's Well That Ends Well* seems to dwell on the distinction between youth and age. E. M. W. Tillyard found in the comedy an "evident dislike of the younger generation,"[5] and it is certainly true that the play's young people—Bertram, Parolles, and Lavache especially—come off a poor second to their elders—the Countess, Lafeu, and the King of France. These latter three, who reflect repeatedly on their advanced age, provide the play with whatever ethical stability it possesses; the Countess, especially, provides a moral anchor for its shifting values.

Shaw called the role of the Countess "the most beautiful old woman's part ever written."[6] Her subtle influence oversees the progress of this comedy's entanglements like a moral compass. Her determined support and virtual adoption of the abandoned Helena serve to ennoble the heroine. Her maternal wisdom, gained through the perspective of age, throws into sharp relief the moral insufficiency of her son, while at the same time suggesting that no child of such a woman could long remain misguided. The recurring presence of the Countess gives assurance that "all's well" or will, at least, end well.

Unfortunately, in dramaturgical terms all does not end well. The fifth act of this play is one of the poorest in Shakespeare. In an attempt to create theatrical effect, the dramatist introduced a number of arbitrary developments and protracted the suspense of Helena's final appearance beyond what is serviceable or credible. We are suddenly apprised of a daughter to Lafeu, never before mentioned, to whom Bertram is now betrothed. The King's ring emerges abruptly as a plot element also hitherto unmentioned, and Bertram confronts and besmears the supposedly defiled Diana, who claims him for her husband. These are the trappings of second-rate melodrama.

Bertram's succession of desperate lies regarding his possession of the King's ring, his seduction of Diana, and his false accusation of her as a common prostitute serves only to complicate his character at the very moment when he should be ennobled, in preparation for his reunion with the virtuous Helena. Consequently, the final joining of Bertram and Helena is artificial, perfunctory, and void of any sense of personal reconciliation. At best it affirms abstract and symbolic values such as mercy, forgiveness, repentance, and the like. But this sort of finale Shakespeare was to accomplish far more effectively in his last romances—especially *The Winter's Tale* and *The Tempest*.

The stage history of *All's Well That Ends Well* is brief and undistinguished. There is no record of its having been performed before 1741, when it was staged at Goodman's Fields Theatre. It appeared at the Theatre Royal, Drury Lane, in the following year and again in 1794, when John Philip Kemble produced it and played Bertram. In 1832 an operatic version was given at Covent Garden.

More recently, the comedy was first played at Stratford-upon-Avon in 1916, and William Poel's Elizabethan Stage Society produced it in 1920. There have been no notable professional productions of it in America, except for those staged by companies that devote themselves to the entire Shakespeare canon. Even then, *All's Well That Ends Well* seems never to be very attractive to modern audiences, for reasons that are not difficult to appreciate. It is one of Shakespeare's least admirable comedies.

Measure for Measure

Measure for Measure is the best and most stageworthy of Shakespeare's three problem comedies. Like *Troilus and Cressida*, it utilizes a seamy setting and some dissolute characters to create a dark and unpleasant atmosphere. Like *All's Well That Ends Well*, its action depends upon a degree of implausible folktale plot material. But unlike either of those plays, *Measure for Measure* presents fully credible, psychologically complex characters involved in ethical predicaments that engage and sustain our interest. The play contains some of the finest acting scenes in Shakespeare (for example, the two Angelo-Isabella interviews of II, ii and iv, and the Isabella-Claudio scene in III, i).

Shakespeare's principal source was an earlier play, *Promos and Cassandra* (1578), by George Whetstone. From it he took the situation that dominates the first half of the play: Isabella's dilemma in choosing between her chastity and her brother's life. The working out of Isabella's problem, which dominates the action from the middle of Act III, scene i, to the end, is largely Shakespeare's original plotting. The Viennese setting, too, with its moral disintegration and low life (Lucio,

Pompey, Mistress Overdone, and friends), is Shakespeare's invention and is vital to the plot in setting Isabella's virtue in sharp relief.

The "bed trick" (the substitution of Mariana for Isabella in Angelo's bed) Shakespeare borrowed from his own *All's Well That Ends Well*. This device, and that of the benign ruler going in disguise among his people to observe them, were folktale ingredients, handed down from the Middle Ages. It is the intrusion of these typical intrigue-plot materials upon the Isabella-Angelo involvement that causes problems in the overall effect of this dark comedy.

Measure for Measure is not wholly consistent in plotting, style, or language. The first half, dominated by Angelo, Isabella, and Claudio, contains some of Shakespeare's most realistic blank verse and some of his finest characterizing. Its people are wholly credible and their involvement is compelling, presented almost at the level of psychological realism. The language, tone, and action shift abruptly, however, with the Duke's interruption of the Claudio-Isabella scene in Act III, scene i.

The intervention of the Duke and the resultant shift in emphasis are dramatically necessary, because the Isabella-Angelo problem, if allowed to work itself out, would lead to a tragic conclusion. Isabella must, after all, make the choice either to submit to Angelo's lust (thereby damning her soul and effecting a decidedly unhappy denouement) or to seal her brother's death warrant. The dilemma that Shakespeare created and explored so beautifully is insoluble, save for the Duke's intervention.

Thus, the Duke breaks off Isabella's denunciation of Claudio's cowardice; the powerfully emotive verse shifts to businesslike prose; and the action becomes that of an intrigue comedy. Plotting and "practicing," accompanied by low-comedy relief, become the predominant stuff of the play's second half. We are asked to focus on the character of the Duke as he, in the disguise of Friar, guides the other characters safely through the perils of the plot to the happy ending. The play's second half, although more complicated and intriguing than the first, is somehow less emotionally satisfying, for our intense interest in Isabella's dilemma is diverted.

The character of Isabella has long been the cause of much critical debate. Those who disparage her find her at best inconsistent, at worst morally reprehensible in her "rancid chastity." Sir Arthur Quiller-Couch, in his introduction to the New Cambridge edition, saw an inconsistency in Isabella's prizing of her own chastity while at the same time serving as a "bare procuress" in bringing Mariana to Angelo's bed. He accused her of being "chaste, even fiercely chaste, for herself, without quite knowing what chastity means." Other critics have similarly deplored the woman's willingness to let her brother die merely to preserve her virginity.

Isabella, however, is neither inconsistent nor morally wrongheaded. In allowing Mariana to substitute for herself in Angelo's bed, Isabella is following the imperative of the Duke, who, in his disguise of Friar, represents ecclesiastical authority. (To the audience, aware of his true identity, he represents civil authority as well.) More importantly, for Shakespeare's audience Mariana has every right to Angelo's bed. A betrothal, or troth-plight, was legally binding and tantamount to marriage, including the conjugal rights thereof. Angelo had betrayed Mariana in breaking off the marriage, and she was fully justified in forcing him to honor his commitment. The Duke, as Friar, makes this quite clear:

> Nor, gentle daughter, fear you not at all.
> He is your husband on a pre-contract:

> To bring you thus together, 'tis no sin,
> Sith that the justice of your title to him
> Doth flourish the deceit.
>
> (IV, i)

To accuse Isabella of procuring is to fail to understand the convention of betrothal.

The problem of Isabella's readiness to sacrifice Claudio to her chastity is more difficult. Her behavior is certainly extreme, particularly to a modern audience, but we must remember that she was a novice, about to take her vows, and was in fact called from the nunnery to aid Claudio. Her virtue is emphasized throughout the play; even the licentious Lucio calls her "a thing ensky'd and sainted" (I, iv). She believes deeply that to submit to Angelo would damn her soul. Thus steeped in religious teaching, she must choose between corporeal life (Claudio's) and the life everlasting (her own):

> Better it were a brother died at once,
> Than that a sister, by redeeming him,
> Should die for ever.
> . . . .
> Then, Isabel, live chaste, and, brother, die:
> More than our brother is our chastity.
>
> (II, iv)

It is possible, of course, to interpret Isabella also in the light of modern psychology. It is not difficult to see in her a woman neurotically terrified of sex. Why had she chosen a nun's life in the first place? Her denunciation of Claudio, when he pleads for her help, is hysterical:

> O you beast!
> O faithless coward! O dishonest wretch!
> Wilt thou be made a man out of my vice?

Is't not a kind of incest, to take life
From thine own sister's shame?
. . . .
                  Take my defiance!
Die, perish!

                              (III, i)

Isabella is, then, a wholly consistent, psychologically credible character—at least, throughout the first part of the play. After the shift to prose at Act III, scene i, she becomes less interesting than she is in her scenes with Claudio and Angelo—more a pawn in the Duke's stratagem.

Angelo is a similarly engaging and multifaceted character, and he remains so until the very end. Angelo is overzealous in his determination to make an example of Claudio's fornication. As Lucio points out:

> The vice is of a great kindred; it is well allied: but it is impossible to extirp it quite, friar, till eating and drinking be put down. . . . Why, what a ruthless thing is this in him [Angelo], for the rebellion of a codpiece to take away the life of a man!
>
>   (III, ii)

Angelo's excessive zeal becomes even more apparent when we understand that Claudio's "crime" is hardly that at all. His status with Julietta is precisely what Angelo's had been with Mariana. Since Claudio and Julietta were betrothed, Claudio's fornication is an offense only in a technical sense. The Provost, a voice of reason in Vienna's court, points out that Claudio "hath but as offended in a dream" (II, ii). Claudio tells Lucio:

>   Upon a true contract
> I got possession of Julietta's bed:
> You know the lady; she is fast my wife,

> Save that we do the denunciation lack
> Of outward order.
>
> (I, ii)

One can make a case against Angelo also in his choosing to enforce a law that had lain unobserved for nineteen years and then arbitrarily making an example of Claudio when Vienna, we are clearly shown, is full of fornicators. Claudio's resentment is justified:

> But this new governor
> Awakes me all the enrolled penalties
> Which have, like unscour'd armour, hung by
> the wall
> So long that nineteen zodiacs have gone round
> And none of them been worn; and, for a name,
> Now puts the drowsy and neglected act
> Freshly on me: 'tis surely for a name.
>
> (I, ii)

Angelo's motives and zeal are certainly questionable, but he is no villain. He is basically a sympathetic character, notwithstanding his attempt to seduce Isabella. A man who has long suppressed all natural feeling—who "scarce confesses/That his blood flows" (I, iii)—he is confused and ashamed when lust overwhelms him, as his soliloquy at the end of Act II, scene ii, attests:

> O, fie, fie, fie!
> What dost thou, or what art thou, Angelo?
> Dost thou desire her foully for those things
> That make her good?
> . . . .
> Never could the strumpet,
> With all her double vigour, art and nature,
> Once stir my temper; but this virtuous maid
> Subdues me quite.

His confusion, shame, and helplessness are genuine.

Because Shakespeare has drawn Angelo with sympathy we can understand, if not condone, his deplorable behavior in trying to seduce Isabella and, after having done so (as he thinks), ordering Claudio's execution to proceed. Angelo, "though angel on the outward side" (III, ii), is morally weak within and strangely moving in his weakness. Shakespeare depicted him as a man deeply in need of forgiveness, and that is precisely what he gets in the final scene, thanks to the maneuvering of the Duke.

Some of the problems in this problem comedy derive from Shakespeare's characterization of the Duke, who can be seen to function on at least three separate levels —the realistic, the intrigue-conventional, and the symbolic. Shakespeare's intention in respect to the Duke is not entirely clear.

As a realistic character, the Duke Vincentio is flawed. His objectives and motivations are at best ambiguous, at worst heartless. He abdicates his responsibilities as ruler of Vienna, presumably having lost his ability to govern effectively. The city has become a cesspool of immorality, overrun with bawds, pimps, and prostitutes. The Duke admits that this situation is directly due to his laxity:

> We have strict statutes and most biting laws,
> The needful bits and curbs to headstrong
>   weeds,
> Which for this nineteen years we have let slip;
> . . . .
>   So our decrees,
> Dead to infliction, to themselves are dead;
> And liberty plucks justice by the nose;
> The baby beats the nurse, and quite athwart
> Goes all decorum.
>
> (I, iii)

He therefore pretends to leave Vienna, bestowing full authority for cleaning up the city on Angelo, a strict moralist "whose blood/Is very snow-broth" (I, iv). One can question the Duke's wisdom in his choice of a deputy. Although he praises Angelo's moral stringency in the opening scene, we learn later (III, i) that he has, all along, been fully aware of Angelo's past betrayal of the unfortunate Mariana. Angelo has repudiated his betrothal and "swallowed his vows whole, pretending in her [Mariana] discoveries of dishonor." Yet this is the man the Duke chooses to cleanse Vienna.

Much of the Duke's behavior is indefensible at the level of realism. He behaves heartlessly in allowing Angelo to proceed with his attempted seduction of Isabella. Fully aware of Angelo's lascivious intentions, the Duke not only fails to intervene but also, in his role of Friar, instructs Claudio to abandon all hope and prepare for death. This bit of unfeeling deception is accomplished through an outright lie:

> Angelo had never the purpose to corrupt her; only he hath made an assay of her virtue to practise his judgement with the disposition of natures: she . . . hath made him that gracious denial which he is most glad to receive. I am confessor to Angelo, and I know this to be true.
> (III, i)

Again acting with seeming cruelty, the Duke allows Isabella to believe that Claudio has indeed been executed (IV, iii), even though he knows this to be untrue. Viewed as a realistic character, in the same category with Angelo, Claudio, and Isabella, the Duke is an unfeeling, duplicitous, eavesdropping trickster. Surely this was not Shakespeare's intention.

Many of the Duke's actions after Act III, scene i, make sense when we view him as the conventional "practicer" of an intrigue plot. As such, he is a stage manager for the events of the play's second half, and his disguise is the dramatic device that allows him to function in this role. As Friar, he can gain access to any of the play's characters and practice his deceptions undiscovered. It is the Friar who suggests to Isabella the bed trick, convinces Mariana to substitute for the assignation with Angelo, arranges the substitution of Ragozine's head for Claudio's, and so on. As Friar, also, the Duke can encourage Lucio to slander him to his face (III, ii; IV, iii), thus adding some much-needed comic relief to the play's second half.

As a conventional "practicer," then, the Duke/Friar character obviously is indispensable to the movement of the plot. He designs its intrigues, oversees their execution, and brings about the happy resolution of a potentially tragic action. Still, it is obvious that Shakespeare intended a more significant role than that of mere intriguer for Vincentio, Duke of Vienna.

It is at the symbolic level that the role of the Duke is most significant, for this play has its share of allegorical implications. It has, in fact, been linked to the English morality-play tradition by some critics. Abstract concepts like justice, mercy, repentance, and forgiveness become embodied in the actions of its characters, and the Duke is the motive force, "like power divine," that manages the allegory. As Duke he is head of state. As Friar he is spokesman for the Church. As a dramatic character he unites the functions of Church and State—dispensing justice, tempering it with mercy, and effecting forgiveness for the repentant Angelo. All of this coalesces in the comedy's long final scene (V, i).

Many of the Duke's actions, troubling at the level of realism, become comprehensible if we see him as a symbol of benevolent authority—a teacher of the other characters. Although they may suffer, those who put their trust in his wisdom and authority learn valuable lessons and are ultimately made happy. Isabella's chastity is preserved, Claudio's life is spared, and

Mariana gains her rightful husband. Those who defy this same authority are dealt with accordingly; Lucio the whoremaster, slanderer of the Duke, is condemned to marry his "punk."

Angelo's fate is not so simple. He is required to wed Mariana, the woman he dishonored, and he is condemned to answer for Claudio's supposed death with his own life. In the Duke's words:

> The very mercy of the law cries out
> Most audible, even from his proper tongue,
> "An Angelo for Claudio, death for death!"
> Haste still pays haste, and leisure answers
>   leisure;
> Like doth quit like, and MEASURE still FOR
>   MEASURE.
>
> (V, i)

The Duke thus applies to Angelo the same legalistic, eye-for-an-eye concept of justice that the latter had applied in condemning Claudio to death.

But Angelo must not die. We the audience, as well as the Duke, know that Claudio is alive and that Angelo is innocent of murder. The others are ignorant of this fact. The Duke could simply reveal Claudio and put an end to Angelo's painful remorse, but the allegory must work itself out. The Duke must temper justice with mercy—but with mercy earned through Isabella's suffering and ultimate forgiveness of her persecutor. For the Duke to forgive Angelo would be meaningless, since Claudio lives and the Duke knows it; there is nothing for him to forgive. But Isabella's forgiveness will be of the true metal, for she must plead for the life of her brother's supposed murderer. This she does:

> Most bounteous sir, (*Kneeling.*)
> Look if it please you, on this man condemn'd,
> As if my brother lived: I partly think
> A due sincerity govern'd his deeds,

Till he did look on me: since it is so,
Let him not die. My brother had but justice,
In that he did the thing for which he died:
For Angelo,
His act did not o'ertake his bad intent,
And must be buried but as an intent
That perish'd by the way.

(V, i)

This is the supreme moment in the play's thematic system—the moment toward which the Duke had been working all along. Through the omniscience of the Duke and his ministrations as moral mentor, the repentant Angelo learns the meaning of mercy and Isabella learns what it is to forgive. Both characters must arrive at these truths at the cost of considerable suffering, but both are ennobled by it. And their mutual enlightenment, so Christian in its implications, brings about the "resurrection" of Claudio—the ultimate bestowal of grace on both Angelo and Isabella.

The effect of the comedy's closing moments is entirely satisfying, but our satisfaction derives not from the personal reconciliation of the play's characters at the level of realism. It is significant that, upon Claudio's unmasking, neither he, Angelo, nor Isabella has another word to say. Shakespeare has denied us the tearful reunion—the personal reactions and emotional speeches that we would find in a wholly realistic comedy. The effect of this is to direct our attention to the allegorical implications of what has occurred; we are invited to contemplate the universal significance of the action. Thus, the Duke summarily ties up the loose ends, banters briefly with Lucio, and ends the play.

Measure for Measure has been a fairly popular play in the theater. It works better on stage than it does in the reading, and it has often been produced with considerable success. It was repeatedly performed

Angelo (Jonathan Pryce, left) and Lucio (John Nettles), from the 1978 production of *Measure for Measure* at the Royal Shakespeare Theatre at Stratford-upon-Avon. Director, Barry Kyle; designer, Christopher Morley.

during the eighteenth century, with such famous actresses as Mrs. Bracegirdle, Mrs. Cibber, Peg Woffington, and the great Sarah Siddons triumphing as Isabella.

The comedy was less frequently played during the nineteenth century, possibly because its coarse sexuality offended Victorian sensibilities. William Charles Macready had success as the Duke in his 1824 production, as did Samuel Phelps at Sadler's Wells in 1846. William Poel's Elizabethan Stage Society mounted an 1895 version on an exact replica of the stage of the Fortune Theatre of Shakespeare's London. Poel himself played Angelo.

More recently, Tyrone Guthrie directed a version of *Measure for Measure* for the Old Vic in 1933, with Charles Laughton earning rave reviews as Angelo. Peter Brook directed a successful version for the Shakespeare Memorial Theatre at Stratford-upon-Avon in 1950. A comment on that production by Kenneth Tynan suggests the theatrical power inherent in *Measure for Measure*, when well directed and well acted:

> Brook's triumph . . . is his fifth act: a scene of such coincidences and lengthy impossibilities, such forced reconciliations and incredible cruelties that most producers flog it through at breakneck speed towards the welcome curtain. Fully aware of the tension his flawless timing has created, Brook here has the effrontery to sit down and let it ride: into this dreadful act he inserts half a dozen long pauses, working up a new miracle of tension which Shakespeare knew nothing about. The thirty-five seconds of dead silence which elapse before Isabella decides to make her plea for Angelo's life were a long, prickly moment of doubt which had every heart in the theatre thudding.[1]

Pericles, Prince of Tyre

Shakespeare's last four comedies—*Pericles*, *Cymbeline*, *The Winter's Tale*, and *The Tempest*—are frequently compared for their shared characteristics of tragicomic romance. In *Pericles*, the earliest of the four, Shakespeare seems largely to have experimented with the themes and dramatic ideas that he was to develop with greater skill in the latter three. *Pericles*, a rather poor play (and of questionable authorship), is of interest mainly for its promise of better things to come.

Written probably between 1606 and 1608, *Pericles* is based upon the well-known legend of Apollonius of Tyre. This popular tale of shipwrecks, separations, and royal familial reunions dates back to the fifth or sixth century and is known to have existed in at least a hundred versions by the time Shakespeare put pen to *Pericles*. He had drawn upon the same legend earlier for *The Comedy of Errors* and *Twelfth Night* and was to do so again for his final three romances.

Shakespeare's immediate sources for the Apollonius legend were two versions by John Gower (1325?–1408) and Lawrence Twyne (fl. 1576), the former's *Confessio Amantis* and the latter's *Patterne of Paynfull*

Aduentures. The Gower work was particularly influential, and Shakespeare included in *Pericles* a chorus figure who is meant to represent the medieval poet himself, telling his own tale.

Shakespeare's precise role in the authorship of *Pericles* has never been satisfactorily determined. Critics do agree that the play is neither originally nor wholly his creation. Although it appeared in a number of quarto printings with Shakespeare's name affixed to the title pages, *Pericles* was not included in the First Folio of 1623, for reasons that can only be guessed at. One theory is that the Folio editors knew for certain that the play was not wholly Shakespeare's. It was not until Malone's edition of Shakespeare in 1790 that *Pericles* became generally accepted in the Shakespeare canon.

It is most probable that *Pericles* represents Shakespeare's reworking of an earlier play by another author (Thomas Heywood has been suggested) and that Acts I and II are almost totally free of Shakespeare's influence. It is only Acts III–V that exhibit passages unmistakably the Bard's, as witnessed by their tighter structure, their language and versification, and their realistic prose passages (the brothel scenes of Act IV especially).

Pericles defies almost every principle of dramatic construction. It is highly episodic and cast in a form essentially narrative rather than dramatic. Much of the story's action is told to us by the narrator Gower, and what we see enacted through the dialogue is a series of loosely connected episodes, some of which are of less dramatic interest than those events merely narrated or pantomimed in dumb show.

Shakespeare had used the convention of the chorus/ narrator before in plays such as *Romeo and Juliet* and *Henry V*, but never to the extent found in *Pericles*. Gower is a dominant figure here, appearing eight times and speaking some 300 lines of verse. Much of the Pericles saga is told by Gower, whose archaic diction and rhymed verse passages (both iambic pentameter and iambic tetrameter) serve to shift locales and jump spans of time in the narrative. Gower's role also contributes to the fairy-tale quality of the action. *Pericles*, unlike any other of Shakespeare's comedies, is little more than illustrated storytelling—childlike in its simplicity and directness.

There is a singular lack of causality in the string of episodes that constitutes the plot of *Pericles*. A given scene does not necessarily result from previous action; it simply follows it. For example, Act I is concerned with Pericles' discovery of the incestuous relationship of King Antiochus with his daughter, an intrigue that has no bearing upon subsequent action. The incestuous pair never again appear after Act I, and Pericles leaves Antioch behind. Moreover, Antiochus commands Thaliard to murder Pericles, and Thaliard goes to Tyre, ostensibly to do so. But upon learning of Pericles' flight to Tarsus, Thaliard abandons pursuit and disappears from the play. The entire first act of *Pericles* could be omitted, with no harm done to the clarity of the remaining story. (The play was thus produced, in fact, at Stratford-upon-Avon in 1947; Paul Scofield was Pericles.)

In addition to its haphazard structure, *Pericles* includes frequent improbabilities and absurdities in plotting. We are asked to believe, for example, that many suitors to the daughter of Antiochus have failed to divine the meaning of the King's riddle. Pericles alone is wise enough to solve it. But the riddle is absurdly transparent and its meaning is clear:

> I am no viper, yet I feed
> On mother's flesh which did me breed.

I sought a husband, in which labour
I found that kindness in a father:
He's father, son, and husband mild;
I mother, wife, and yet his child.
How they may be, and yet in two,
As you will live, resolve it you.

(I, i)

Furthermore, it makes no sense that Antiochus would embody in his riddle evidence of the very sin he wished to conceal. The entire riddle business is inherited from traditional folklore and is simply transcribed from the source story; it is not made dramatically credible within the plot.

There are additional improbabilities. Why does Antiochus, knowing that Pericles has discovered his sin, extend a forty-day reprieve to the prince, allowing him to escape? Why does Pericles, whose stated purpose was to flee the murderous Thaliard, suddenly arrive at Tarsus with an argosy of food for the starving populace? Why, once arrived at Pentapolis, does Pericles conceal his royal lineage and pretend to be a humble knight? These are but a few of the questions that might be asked about the childlike, fairy-tale narrative embodied in the plot of *Pericles*. This is simple fare, meant, in Gower's words, merely "to glad your ear, and please your eyes" (Prologue).

The heart of Pericles' story is his marriage to Thaisa, his subsequent loss of both her and their infant daughter, and his eventual reunion with the two women some fourteen years later. This is the narrative that commences with Act II; its only connection with the first act is the introduction there of Cleon and Dionyza of Tarsus. The story is told in direct-line narrative. There is no central conflict; *Pericles* is almost totally free of character struggle and opposition.

The action is kept going by the influence of fate—
"Fortune" and "the gods." The human characters are
mere sufferers at the mercy of supernatural forces.

Pericles is the central figure of this play. The plot
is, in fact, a biography of Pericles, in the epic
narrative tradition. (The similarity to Homer's
Odyssey has often been noted.) But as a Shakespeare
hero, Pericles is unique. He is a passive figure who
patiently suffers the trials with which Fortune afflicts
him. He is a wholly good character, without flaw or
failings, and does nothing to bring misfortune upon
himself. Nor does he struggle in the face of adversity.
Pericles is, in the words of Bertrand Evans, "Shakespeare's only entirely will-less hero."[1]

We first see this quality of unquestioning resignation in Pericles when he is washed up on the shores of
Pentapolis (II, i), after enduring the first of three
tempests that occur in the course of the play:

> Yet cease your ire, you angry stars of heaven!
> Wind, rain, and thunder, remember, earthly
>   man
> Is but a substance that must yield to you.
> . . . .
> Let it suffice the greatness of your powers
> To have bereft a prince of all his fortunes;
> And having thrown him from your watery
>   grave,
> Here to have death in peace is all he'll crave.

One remembers, by contrast, Lear's defiance of *his*
tempest: "Blow, winds, and crack your cheeks! rage!
blow! . . . Rumble thy bellyful! Spit, fire! spout, rain!"
Pericles is quite a different king and seems content to
play the helpless victim of Nature's rage.

When the three fishermen, in the same scene, come
upon the waterlogged prince ("*Enter* Pericles, *wet*"),
he describes himself to them as

> A man whom both the waters and the wind,
> In that vast tennis-court, have made the ball
> For them to play upon.

Again, we hear an echo from *King Lear*: "As flies to wanton boys, are we to the gods,/They kill us for their sport."

Pericles' passivity is evident later in the way in which he becomes wed to Thaisa. In no sense does he court the princess; his only aggressive act is to participate in the knights' tournament. Thaisa makes the advances, presenting him with the victor's wreath (II, iii). She chooses him for her favorite, sensing some nobility beneath his poor exterior: "To me he seems like diamond to glass." In Act II, scene v, Simonides virtually commands the two to marry and Pericles passively accepts the commission, calling himself "A stranger and distressed gentleman,/That never aim'd so high to love your daughter."

Finally, Pericles exhibits the ultimate in passivity when, believing his daughter dead (IV, iv), he withdraws from human society for fourteen years, refusing even to speak or groom himself. Robbed of its central figure, the narrative turns at that point to its secondary figure, Marina.

Beginning with Act IV, a good deal of the focus shifts to the daughter of Pericles and Thaisa, now grown into a beautiful and wholly virtuous teenager. Like Pericles, Marina suffers extreme misfortune through no fault of her own and despite her consummate goodness. Like Pericles also, her character is idealized; she is purity personified:

> I never spake bad word, nor did ill turn
> To any living creature: believe me, la,
> I never kill'd a mouse, nor hurt a fly:
> I trod upon a worm against my will,
> But I wept for it.
>
> (IV, i)

Unlike Pericles, however, Marina exerts some will in determining her own fate.

Marina becomes the intended victim of her foster mother Dionyza, whose character changes abruptly (with the flimsiest of motivation) between Acts III and IV, simply because the story demands it. The quondam kindly queen becomes a wicked murderess, berating her husband (IV, iii) like Lady Macbeth, and ordering Leonine to kill the innocent girl. This bit of fairy-tale skulduggery comes to naught when pirates save Marina's life and sell her to the proprietors of a brothel.

It is in the brothel that Marina actively determines, at least in part, the course of her fate. The brothel scenes (IV, ii, v, and vi), written in realistic prose, sharply contrast the fantasy of the first three acts and furnish the play with what little comic material it possesses. (The fishermen in II, i, provide the only other note of mirth.) Boult, the Pandar, and the Bawd, with their earthy sex jokes and utterly amoral outlook, put one in mind of Lucio and his cohorts in *Measure for Measure*; these scenes are surely Shakespeare's. In them Marina fights for her chastity and reforms her would-be seducer, the lecherous Lysimachus, who eventually leads her to her long-lost father and becomes her husband. This is the sole incident where a major character actively influences the narrative line in *Pericles*; all other shifts in action result from external forces.

The most important of these external forces is the sea. *Pericles* is rich with references to the sea and its unpredictable violence, and the play's three tempests are responsible for the movement of the plot. In *Pericles*, the sea is the ultimate instrument of Fortune, bringing both good and ill to the play's helpless humans.

Pericles' first encounter with the sea finds him shipwrecked and cast up on the shores of Pentapolis. This misfortune is reported by Gower:

> For now the wind begins to blow;
> Thunder above and deeps below
> Make such unquiet, that the ship
> Should house him safe is wreck'd and split.
> . . . .
> Till fortune, tired with doing bad,
> Threw him ashore, to give him glad.
>
> (II, Prologue)

But ill fortune turns to good when this same tempest casts up the suit of armor that had belonged to Pericles' father and allows him to compete in the tournament at King Simonides' court. Pericles acknowledges the sea's unexpected kindness:

> Thanks, fortune, yet, that, after all my crosses,
> Thou givest me somewhat to repair myself;
> . . . .
> My shipwreck now's no ill,
> Since I have here my father's gift in's will.
>
> (II, i)

The second tempest, even more violent and malevolent than the first, is that which causes the death of Thaisa as she gives birth to Pericles' daughter, whom he names Marina for her sea birth. (The grown Marina, mourning her nurse's death in IV, i, observes: "Born in a tempest, . . ./This world to me is like a lasting storm.") Again, Gower describes the storm, but there is also an accompanying shipboard scene, in which the nurse Lychorida brings Pericles both his newborn babe and the news of his queen's death. Pericles' subdued reaction is typical of his resigned attitude throughout: "O you gods!/Why do you make us love your goodly gifts,/And snatch them straight away?" (III, i).

The sailors insist that Thaisa's body be cast overboard in a "caulked and bitumed" chest and Pericles submits to their will. Again the tempest proves both malignant and benign, for the same storm casts Thaisa's coffin up on the shores of Ephesus (the setting, incidentally, of *The Comedy of Errors*), where she is miraculously revived, unbeknownst to Pericles, by the conjurer Cerimon.

The third and final storm that Pericles endures is only briefly mentioned by Gower in Act IV, scene iv. After being told of his daughter's supposed death and shown her monument, Pericles "puts on sackcloth, and to sea. He bears/A tempest, which his mortal vessel tears,/And yet he rides it out." (It may be that this tempest is figurative—internal and personal—rather than literal, for the "mortal vessel" refers to Pericles' body. He "rides out" [survives] his tempestuous grief.) This sea voyage is the one that brings Pericles to Mytilene, the very city where Marina now dwells in an "honest house."

Pericles arrives at Mytilene on a day of festivity; the moving reunion with his long-lost daughter occurs on the day of Neptune's feast. Neptune, god of the seas, has played a central role in the saga of Pericles. As the supreme manipulator of Pericles' and Marina's fates, he sundered them with storms, only to preside over their reunion fourteen years later. Pericles, face to face with Marina and joyful at last, finds expression in sea imagery:

> This great sea of joys rushing upon me
> O'erbear[s] the shores of my mortality,
> And drown[s] me with their sweetness.
>
> (V, i)

The reunion scene between Pericles and Marina is the dramatic highlight of this otherwise somewhat insubstantial comedy. In it we find realized the major themes and patterns of action that were to occupy Shakespeare in his final three romances: plots spanning multiple generations of characters, the restoration of long-severed familial ties, lost and recovered royalty, the healing and conciliatory properties of time, and the advocacy of patience in adversity. In *Pericles* the latter is central to the play's theme.

Pericles is the model of patience. He endures his misfortunes throughout the play with stoical resignation and is at last rewarded with the recovery of his daughter and wife. Marina similarly endures fortune's blows. At their reunion Pericles says of her: "Yet thou dost look/Like Patience gazing on kings' graves, and smiling/Extremity out of act."

After fourteen years of patient endurance, Pericles rejoins the human community, dons once more his royal robes, and, to the accompaniment of celestial music, receives a visit from the goddess Diana. This theophany leads the prince to Diana's temple and to his final joy, the recovery of his wife Thaisa. The sublime spirituality of the last act of *Pericles* is quite moving and nearly redeems the whole. Gower's closing chorus summarizes the significance of the play's action:

> In Pericles, his queen and daughter, [you have]
> seen,
> Although assail'd with fortune fierce and keen,
> Virtue preserved from fell destruction's blast,
> Led on by heaven, and crown'd with joy at
> last.

Modern audiences have few opportunities to see *Pericles* on the stage, for it is seldom produced. In Shakespeare's time, however, it was extremely popular and remained so until the closing of the theaters in 1642. It received six quarto printings between 1609 and 1635—a sure sign of its popularity.

Pericles was the first of Shakespeare's plays to be revived after the restoration of Charles II in 1660. The young actor Thomas Betterton, soon to become the finest actor on the Restoration stage, earned much success in the title role. Thereafter, strangely, the play disappears from theatrical records for almost two hundred years.

Samuel Phelps gave *Pericles* a spectacular revival at Sadler's Wells in 1854, complete with elaborately staged storm scenes. Phelps, who played Pericles himself, emphasized the visual appeal of the play and cut completely Gower's narratives. He also largely expurgated the brothel scenes in compliance with Victorian sensibilities. The production was an enormous success and ran for several weeks.

Since Phelps's production, *Pericles* has been neglected on the professional stage. Robert Atkins's production at the Old Vic in 1921 earned moderate success, and the 1947 version at Stratford-upon-Avon (previously mentioned) was generally praised. The New York Shakespeare Festival mounted a version in Central Park in the summer of 1974.

There are beauties in *Pericles*—especially in its final act—but the play's sparce stage history indicates that Shakespeare was, in his final years, capable of far better. His last three romances were to improve upon the tragicomic style so imperfectly essayed in *Pericles, Prince of Tyre*.

Cymbeline

This play has many just sentiments, some natural dialogues, and some pleasing scenes, but they are obtained at the expense of much incongruity. To remark the folly of the fiction, the absurdity of the conduct, the confusion of the names and manners of different times, and the impossibility of the events in any system of life, were to waste criticism upon unresisting imbecility, upon faults too evident for detection, and too gross for aggravation.

Thus wrote Dr. Samuel Johnson in his *General Observations on the Plays of Shakespeare* (1756) regarding *Cymbeline*, a complex and fanciful work that represents Shakespeare's second attempt at tragicomic romance.

His first effort in the genre had been *Pericles*, but unlike that play, whose farfetched tale of adventures was told with childlike narrative simplicity, *Cymbeline*'s multiple plots and intrigues unfold with elaborate design. Complication is heaped upon complication in a succession of improbabilities and coincidences that can confuse the most attentive reader or theatergoer.

Dr. Johnson's dismay at *Cymbeline* was not without some justification, for it is the most complexly plotted of all Shakespeare's plays.

The drama's complexity, as well as its imperfections, are due to Shakespeare's experimenting with a dramatic form relatively new to him at the time of its composition (probably 1609 or 1610): tragicomic romance. Although he had essayed the style earlier in *Pericles*, that play is not entirely Shakespeare's. His authorship of *Cymbeline*, on the other hand, has been questioned only rarely and only in regard to the dream scene (V, iv). Thus, *Cymbeline* represents a major experiment in form, prompted by a variety of influences.

One such influence was the recent acquisition by Shakespeare's company, the King's Men, of the Blackfriars playhouse, an indoor theater offering opportunities for stage spectacle and lighting effects not available in the outdoor public theater for which he had chiefly written up to this time. This would account for the emphasis upon visual effects in *Cymbeline*—for example, the descent of Jupiter in the dream sequence: "Jupiter *descends in thunder and lightning, sitting upon an eagle: he throws a thunderbolt. The Ghosts fall on their knees.*"

Audience tastes, too, were changing in the first decade of the seventeenth century. The novelty of tragicomedy was beginning to please the public, and it may be that Shakespeare, influenced by the success of writers like Francis Beaumont and John Fletcher, was attempting to cater to the new taste for sensationalism and spectacle. (The similarities between *Cymbeline* and Beaumont and Fletcher's *Philaster* have often been noted, although it is not certain which came first.) *Cymbeline* exhibits all the features of the new tragicomedy, as it propels its leading characters to the brink of death and disaster, only to effect their rescue and happiness in the final scene.

Shakespeare drew upon two principal sources for the plot material of *Cymbeline*, combining native history with Italianate intrigue. The setting and framework of the play derive from Holinshed's *Chronicles* (1578) of Britain (the same section that provided the story of King Lear). From Holinshed come the legendary King Cymbeline and the business of the conflict with Rome, as well as many of the characters' names—Belarius, Guiderius, Arviragus, and others. The wager plot between Posthumus and Iachimo, which dominates the first two acts, derives principally from Boccaccio's *Decameron* (the ninth tale of the second day), a source Shakespeare had used also for *Measure for Measure* and *All's Well That Ends Well*.

The action of *Cymbeline* combines elements of at least three distinct literary traditions: the chronicle or history play, the pastoral, and the romance. The three are fused with considerable ingenuity into a complex, fanciful, and occasionally improbable plot.

Least dominant of the three is the chronicle tradition. Shakespeare was, of course, a master of the history play. His nine plays of the kings of England from Richard II through Henry VIII are the finest of their kind. But in *Cymbeline* we find English history serving as a mere framework for the fictional plot, much as it had in *Macbeth* and *King Lear*.

Cymbeline's refusal to pay the tribute to Caesar sets in motion a political conflict that results in war (V, i–iii), but the political plot is a minor one. The threat of war between Britain and Rome is not established until Act III, scene i, long after the major Posthumus-Imogen plot is under way. From that point forward, the political conflict serves mainly to reinforce the atmosphere of general unrest that pervades the play. The martial theme of dissension, conquest, and imminent death intensifies the potentially tragic tone of *Cymbeline*.

A tragic resolution to the political plot is avoided, however, in keeping with the tragicomic tone. The Romans are defeated and the British triumph (amazingly, without loss of life to a single character). Moreover, both sides actually win, for Cymbeline decides voluntarily to pay the tribute to the defeated Caesar. In the political-historical plot, as in the larger action, harmony and accord are finally achieved. Disparate and conflicting forces are ultimately reconciled.

The pastoral tradition is seen in the Belarius-Guiderius-Arviragus subplot. Shakespeare's chief essay in pastoralism up to this time had been *As You Like It*, and there are similarities between that comedy's pastoral idealism and *Cymbeline*'s. The kindly old Belarius contrasts the court with the natural world, much as Duke Senior had done in the Forest of Arden.

Belarius is more important for providing bucolic atmosphere than for advancing the action. His major contribution to the plot—kidnapping the two young sons of Cymbeline—has ended some twenty years before the play begins. In the present action, he is a mere stick figure who mouths pious platitudes but performs little. The conventional hermit of pastoral romance, he instructs his two adopted sons in the joys of the natural life, a life free from the prominence and duplicity of the court:

> O, this life
> Is nobler than attending for a check,
> Richer than doing nothing for a bauble,
> Prouder than rustling in unpaid-for silk.
> . . . .
> Did you but know the city's usuries
> And felt them knowingly; the art o' the court,
> As hard to leave as keep; whose top to climb
> Is certain falling, or so slippery that
> The fear's as bad as falling.
>
> (III, iii)

It is through Belarius's expository narrative in this scene and his constant remarking upon the upright characters of the young princes that we learn of their background and become convinced of their nobility of spirit. Belarius is a chorus figure whose function is to establish the pastoral atmosphere in *Cymbeline*.

The predominant literary mode of *Cymbeline* is that of the romance, a type of fictional narrative that depicts farfetched adventures and intrigues in remote settings. In the romance, love is the central concern. It is treated as a sublime experience, subjected to tests and trials, and shown ultimately triumphant through the faithful perseverance of the lovers. This is certainly the case in *Cymbeline*, where married fidelity is the chief issue in the major plot. Imogen's virtue is subjected to the most rigorous of tests—her husband's wager with Iachimo—and found durable. Her perfection then becomes the source of all her sufferings. As early as Act II, scene i, the Second Lord establishes the primacy of Imogen's virtue as the essential determinant of a happy denouement:

> The heavens hold firm
> The walls of thy dear honour, keep unshaked
> That temple, thy fair mind, that thou mayst
>   stand,
> To enjoy thy banish'd lord and this great land!

Other trappings of romance also are evident in *Cymbeline*: heroines disguised as boys (Imogen), quests and journeys in the cause of love (Posthumus's banishment, Imogen's travels), familial separations and reunions (Imogen and Posthumus; Cymbeline and his sons), restoration of long-lost royalty (Guiderius and Arviragus), loyal servants (Pisanio), villainous intriguers (Iachimo, Cloten), intervention of the supernatural (Jupiter and the Ghosts of the Leonati),

death-simulating drugs (the Queen's potion), coinci-
dence, and mistaken identity.

All of these elements are combined with considerable
ingenuity in *Cymbeline* to bring about, at the denouement, the triumph of the virtuous and the fall of the
wicked—the sort of poetic justice appropriate to the
romance tradition. Even more importantly, these
diverse elements are fused into a stylistic unity through
the dramatist's innovative treatment of tragicomic
structure.

Shakespeare had, of course, combined comic and
serious material previously in many plays. In *Much
Ado about Nothing*, for example, the villainous plot
against Hero's reputation is relieved by intermittent
high comedy (Beatrice and Benedick) and farcical
nonsense (Dogberry and the Watch). Again, in
Measure for Measure the grim business of Angelo's
assault upon Isabella's virtue is played against alter-
nating scenes of low comedy and bawdry with Lucio
and his cohorts.

Cymbeline, however, exhibits a different approach
to the fusion of the comic and the serious. Whereas
the earlier comedies employ an alternation of the two
styles, in *Cymbeline* the suggestion of the comic is
incorporated into the most potentially tragic events
themselves; the ludicrous becomes an integral part of
the serious. There are no scenes here of comic relief
interspersed with the serious episodes. There is not a
single instance in *Cymbeline* of pure comedy (the
fatuousness of Cloten in I, ii, and II, i, possibly excepted). The method of this play, therefore, is one of
a simultaneity of darkness and lightness that leads an
audience to chuckle, or even laugh outright, at the
very moments when the characters perform the most
dastardly deeds or suffer the deepest distress.

One way in which Shakespeare achieved this tragicomic effect was repeatedly to provide the audience

with information not available to the characters, so that the seemingly tragic is attenuated in our perception of it. For example, the Queen's evil is neutralized from the first by the fact that Imogen sees through her hypocrisy: "O Dissembling courtesy! How fine this tyrant/Can tickle where she wounds!" (I, i). Thus we view the Queen's machinations with comic expectation, since she mistakenly thinks that Imogen is taken in by her. The course of the Queen's villainy is further deflected by the physician Cornelius, who assures us (I, v) that the Queen's "poison" will but "dull and stupify the sense awhile" and that "there is/ No danger in what show of death it makes." Thus, the evil Queen is "fool'd/With a most false effect" and we can smile at her, even though she is drawn not as a comic character but with the studied malevolence of a Richard III or an Iago.

Other actions, crafted from seemingly tragic material, are similarly rendered trigicomic by Shakespeare's art. Iachimo's emergence from the trunk to befoul Imogen's reputation (II, ii) could be an act of dire villainy, exciting our fear and pity for Imogen. But it isn't. We are given no foreknowledge that Iachimo has framed such a plan. He casually asks Imogen (I, vi) to keep a treasure-filled trunk for the night; it is Imogen herself who suggests that she keep it in her own bedroom. Iachimo is given no Machiavellian soliloquy to inform us of his intention, so that his emergence from the trunk is a complete surprise to the audience. The effect of it is almost ludicrous in the playing (a jack-in-the-box?), and our astonishment makes fear impossible.

Iachimo, moreover, in addressing the sleeping Imogen, speaks not like a designing villain but like an adoring admirer. His description of the lovely innocent is couched in lyrical verse and imagery of the most benign sort:

How bravely thou becomest thy bed, fresh lily,
And whiter than the sheets! That I might
touch!
. . . .
                    'Tis her breathing that
Perfumes the chamber thus: the flame o' the
taper
Bows toward her, and would under-peep her
lids,
To see the enclosed lights, now canopied
Under these windows, white and azure laced
With blue of heaven's own tinct.

                                        (II, ii)

One is hard put to believe that this man is executing a
plan to slander the innocent girl, divorce her from her
husband, and—as it turns out—cause a murder plot
to be framed against her. The tragicomic treatment
deprives Iachimo of the stature of a true villain such as
Iago, even though his intentions are every bit as vile.
As Granville-Barker stated: "From the first there is
something fantastic about the fellow, and no tragically-
potent scoundrel, we should be sure, will ever come
out of a trunk."[1]

The death of Cloten (IV, ii) provides another example of the tragicomic method of *Cymbeline*. Else-
where in Shakespeare, there is nothing even faintly
comic about the dismemberment or disfiguration of a
dramatic character (Lavinia's hands and tongue in
Titus Andronicus, the pound of Antonio's flesh in
The Merchant of Venice, Macbeth's severed head),
but the killing of Cloten fairly brings the house down.

The effect is achieved in two ways. First, Cloten
himself prepares us for his death by behaving in an
arrogant, obnoxious fashion to the princely Guiderius,
calling him "slave," "robber," "varlet," "lawbreaker,"
"villain," and "thief." This sets him up for retribution.
But more importantly, it is the matter-of-fact bravado

of Guiderius, who returns from the offstage fight
bearing Cloten's head, that removes the deed from the
realm of the truly tragic:

> This Cloten was a fool, an empty purse;
> There was no money in't: not Hercules
> Could have knock'd out his brains, for he had
>   none.

This is comic rhetoric; Guiderius is a boastful fairy-
tale prince who has slain the dragon. Even more comic
is his plan for disposition of the "dragon's" head:

> I'll throw't into the creek
> Behind our rock; and let it to the sea,
> And tell the fishes he's the queen's son, Cloten:
> That's all I reck.

And when the kindly old Belarius tells us, only seventeen lines later, that the two "princely boys" are "as
gentle/As zephyrs blowing below the violet,/Not
wagging his sweet head," the incongruity of his
assessment and the "wagging head" image clinch the
comedy of Cloten's demise.

Perhaps the finest example of the tragicomic style of
Cymbeline occurs later in this same scene when Imogen
awakes to find the headless corpse of Cloten beside her
and thinks it to be that of her husband Posthumus.
Shakespeare has exploited contrary states of awareness
in character and audience here, to fine dramatic effect.
Our feeling for Imogen is complex; we pity her distress
but, knowing that she is deceived, we cannot share her
grief. It is, after all, the fatuous boob Cloten whose
death she mourns and Posthumus is alive and well. As
if to stretch this discrepancy in awarenesses to the
limit, Shakespeare has Imogen go on at length in her
positive identification of the corpse:

A headless man! The garments of Posthumus!
I know the shape of 's leg: this is his hand;
His foot Mercurial; his Martial thigh;
The brawns of Hercules: but his Jovial face—
Murder in Heaven?—How!—'Tis gone.
. . . .
     O Posthumus! alas,
Where is thy head? where's that? Ay me!
  where's that?

This careful cataloging of the corpse's anatomy is ludicrous, despite Imogen's distress, when we realize that these fine classical comparisons are being wasted on the remains of Cloten. There is something comic, too, in Imogen's systematic progression from the leg and foot, up through the thigh and arms, to the missing head. (Consider also the effect, in the staging, of the stuffed mannequin that must be used for the corpse.)

Finally, a comic perspective is encouraged by the irony of Imogen's repeated accusation that Cloten, in league with Pisanio, is to blame for the corpse beside her. It is a masterful scene in the tragicomic vein. We witness our heroine in the depth of despair, feeling in equal measure sympathy for her distress and comic joy for our superior knowledge that her sorrow is misplaced.

As can be seen, the tragicomic tone of *Cymbeline* asks of us a fairly complex and frequently ambivalent response. We are not presented with a clearcut indication of how we are to respond at any given moment, as we are in pure comedy or in conventional tragedy. The play has frequently been criticized for this. But we should approach *Cymbeline* free of preconceived notions about comedy and tragedy, viewing it as adventurous fiction—much as we approach horror stories, tales of the occult, or science fiction.

Tragicomic romance requires little in depth of characterization, and the characters of *Cymbeline* are, accordingly, simple in conception and economical in execution. With few exceptions, the play is peopled with conventional stereotypes.

Cymbeline's Queen is the wicked stepmother of folklore (Shakespeare's debt to the tale of Snow White has often been noted), and her reported death (V, v) requires no more response from us than a happy: "Ding, dong, the witch is dead!" Her husband the king, who gives his name to the play's title, is a mere figurehead. Although he is King of Britain, his only royal act is to dispense general forgiveness at the play's close: "Pardon's the word to all." When pressed by Caius Lucius for the tribute to Rome, he leaves the negotiations to his wife and stepson. It is the influence of his Queen that leads him to force Cloten upon Imogen and banish Posthumus from Britain. All in all, the henpecked Cymbeline is not much of a ruler. He is the "symbolic king of fairy tale. . . . He is a puppet who never comes to life."[2]

Other characters are similarly one-dimensional. Cloten is a malicious fool, as the Second Lord makes clear to us: "That such a crafty devil as is his mother/ Should yield the world this ass!" (II, i). Only in responding to Caius Lucius (III, i) does Cloten exhibit any common sense. Arviragus and Guiderius are symbols of nobility and bravery, barely distinguishable but for the more aggressive behavior of the latter. We accept their innate royal bearing on trust; it is established in what Belarius says of them more than in anything they do or say. Iachimo is a scheming villain of the Italianate school, although one capable of repentance in the final scene.

Posthumus, the closest thing we have to a hero in this play, is somewhat more fully realized than these symbolic fairy-tale figures, but his characterization is inconsistent. He dominates the play's first two acts and is presented there as the epitome of courtly manhood.

The First Gentleman of the opening scene tells us what he is:

> a creature such
> As, to seek through the regions of the earth
> For one his like, there would be something
>   failing
> In him that should compare. I do not think
> So fair an outward and such stuff within
> Endows a man but he.

Despite his heroic domination of the first two acts, however, Posthumus disappears from the play completely during Acts III and IV. When he reappears, after an absence of twelve scenes, he is almost a different character. In the play's final act he is a passive figure, except for his participation in the dumb-show battle scenes. Essentially a chorus figure (V, i; V, iii), a sleeping dreamer (V, iv), and a passive observer of the plot's disentanglements (V, v), the Posthumus of Act V occupies the background of the tapestry, giving way to the play's central figure, Imogen.

The role of Imogen has long been the major attraction in *Cymbeline* for readers, critics, and theatergoers alike. She is the only fully realized character in the play, and she emerges as a woman of charm, strength, ingenuity, and courage. Nineteenth-century commentators especially found Imogen a blessed relief from the picture-book stereotypes of the play's other figures. M. R. Ridley saw Imogen as the "rarest, the most perfect piece of womanhood" in all Shakespeare,[3] and Swinburne called her the "woman best beloved in all the world of song and all the tide of time."[4]

In Imogen, Shakespeare seems to have combined the most attractive elements of a number of his earlier heroines. In her assertiveness with the male sex (especially Cloten) and her ready wit she recalls Beatrice (*Much Ado about Nothing*). Her resourcefulness and self-sufficiency in coping with her masculine disguise in the pastoral setting remind us of Rosalind (*As You Like It*). There are echoes of Desdemona (*Othello*) as she stoically plays the wronged wife. And her refusal to cater to her father's wrongheadedness links her to Cordelia (*King Lear*). Imogen provides a capstone in Shakespeare's gallery of feminine portraiture.

The final scene of *Cymbeline* is astonishing in its technical virtuosity. Shakespeare assembles all the characters and unresolved plot materials of the previous four acts—the disguises, misunderstandings, and intrigues—and brings the action to a close by effecting a series of no fewer than thirteen major discoveries. Moreover, not one of the many characters on the stage is aware of all the facts concerning the past events, disguises, and true identities. Only the audience is in command of all this information, so that the scene and its multiple discoveries are laden with dramatic irony. We watch the wonder of it all from an omniscient vantage point. The denouement of *Cymbeline* is the most complex in Shakespeare.

Since *Cymbeline* presents a tale filled with surprises, unexpected turns of events, and amazing coincidences, its chief appeal is in its ingenuity, complexity, and theatricality. This is not to say, however, that the play is devoid of thought. There are a number of themes (too many for full discussion here) that attest to Shakespeare's seriousness of purpose in creating *Cymbeline*. The play embodies ideas common to the four late romances—ideas concerned with reconciliation, regeneration, repentance, and forgiveness.

Additionally, however, there is a dominant theme unique to *Cymbeline*: the discrepancy between seeming and substance in human conduct. The play repeatedly contrasts external appearances with inward reality. This theme is most concretely set forth in the counterposing of Posthumus and Cloten as opposites—

the former possessing a congruity of inward and outward features, the latter presenting a facade of deceptive seeming.

The "seeming" theme is anticipated in the play's opening speech, where we learn that Cymbeline's entire court, acquiescing to the king's banishment of Posthumus, "wear their faces to the bent/Of the king's looks," pretending to approve of the banishment but secretly favoring the worthy Posthumus over the devious Cloten. Thus, Cymbeline's court is characterized at once by hypocrisy. The First Gentleman then avers that Posthumus's "so fair an outward" accords perfectly with the "stuff within." Philario assures us that Posthumus's material wealth "makes him both without and within" (I, iv). By contrast, whatever material advantages Cloten enjoys seem only to intensify his inner hatefulness, no matter how they enhance his exterior.

The inward-outward paradox of Cloten vis-à-vis Posthumus becomes most concrete in the symbol of clothing. Imogen establishes this in repulsing Cloten:

> His [Posthumus's] meanest garment,
> That ever hath but clipp'd his body, is dearer
> In my respect than all the hairs above thee,
> Were they all made such men.
>
> (II, iii)

Cloten, outraged at the insult, indignantly repeats "his garment!" and "his meanest garment!" four times, before exiting in high dudgeon. And when he comes to plot his rape of the hapless Imogen (III, v), Cloten recalls the insult:

> She said upon a time . . . that she held the very garment of Posthumus in more respect than my noble and natural person [again, Cloten's con-

cern with outward signs]. . . . With that suit
upon my back, will I ravish her.

And with that suit upon his back he gets his head
chopped off—a wonderfully ironic touch.

As the converse to Cloten's donning Posthumus's
clothing, the latter, returning to Britain to defend his
country against the invading Romans (V, i), casts off
his fancy Italianate garb in favor of a humble peasant
costume:

> I'll disrobe me
> Of these Italian weeds and suit myself
> As does a Briton peasant.
> . . . .
> Let me make men know
> More valour in me than my habits show.

Thus does Posthumus, in proving his martial valor,
display "less without and more within." It is the
reverse of Cloten's situation; a humble seeming belies
the strength within. This is but one example of Shakespeare's advancing of thematic material in *Cymbeline*.

Cymbeline is a play that works far better in the
theater than in the reading. Much of its success depends
upon visual effects, and the presence of living actors
serves to flesh out its lightly sketched stereotypes. Its
stage career has been a relatively successful one.

Cymbeline is known to have been played before
Charles I in 1633, but after the Restoration it was
supplanted by an inferior adaptation by Thomas
D'Urfey, *The Injured Princess; or, The Fatal Wager*,
which held the stage from 1682 until 1744. In that year
Shakespeare's original was played at London's Haymarket theater. David Garrick played Posthumus in a
1761 production at Drury Lane and it was one of his
best roles.

The outstanding production of *Cymbeline* in the nineteenth century was that of Henry Irving in 1896. Irving as Iachimo and Ellen Terry as Imogen played to full houses for many weeks. Indeed, Terry was probably one of the greatest of Imogens, to judge by her reviews.

In our own century the play has been staged infrequently but always with some degree of success. Sybil Thorndike made an effective Imogen at the Old Vic in 1918, as did Peggy Ashcroft at the same theater in 1932, accompanied by Anthony Quayle as Caius Lucius and Alastair Sim as the king. In 1937 the Embassy Theatre in London offered a version for which George Bernard Shaw, never one to consider himself inferior to the Bard, rewrote the entire fifth act.

The first American production of *Cymbeline* was that by Lewis Hallam and David Douglass in 1767. It played in both Philadelphia and New York. Some of the great American Imogens have been Fanny Davenport (1880), Helen Modjeska (1882), Julia Marlowe (1891), and Viola Allen (1906). Whenever *Cymbeline* is played, the success of the production inevitably depends upon its Imogen, one of Shakespeare's finer character creations.

The Winter's Tale

In *The Winter's Tale* (1610–11) Shakespeare brought to near perfection the form of tragicomic romance—the genre with which he had been experimenting in *Pericles* and *Cymbeline*. This play is the most successful of the three, particularly in terms of theatrical viability. *The Winter's Tale* can be a deeply affecting work on the stage when well acted and directed with sensitivity.

Shakespeare's source for this play was a fictional romance by Robert Greene called *Pandosto, the Triumph of Time*, published in 1588. It provided the basic ingredients that Shakespeare required in fashioning his tragicomic plot: the oracle of Apollo, a shipwreck, an abandoned infant of royal blood, recovery of lost royalty, and so on. Many such elements appear also in *Pericles* and *Cymbeline*, but never in those plays with the degree of narrative credibility, structural unity, and theatrical power as are found in this play. *The Winter's Tale* is romantic in the best Elizabethan sense of the word, "dealing with love in people of high estate, events controlled by supernatural agency and by chance, and heroic adventure in both courtly and arcadian settings."[1]

The play's title provides a clue as to the sort of story we can expect. A "winter's tale" is an old wives' tale—a story of perilous adventures, of "sprites and goblins," told but to while away a winter's evening. And as the young prince Mamillius tells us: "A sad tale's best for winter" (II, i). Ultimately, of course, the tale ends happily, but it contains considerable sadness along the way, including the death of Mamillius himself.

It is the nature of the genre that tragicomic romance necessarily includes some rather implausible and even farfetched story elements, and critics have been quick to point out this play's shortcomings in that respect. How, for example, could Paulina have successfully hidden Hermione away for sixteen years? Why does Hermione say that Paulina told her of the oracle (V, iii) when she herself had heard it read (III, ii)? How can we accept the anachronisms of the Emperor of Russia and the Renaissance painter Julio Romano in a pre-Christian setting? And should not Shakespeare have known that Bohemia has no seacoast? All of these "defects" are, of course, trivial. Such minor inconsistencies may emerge in the reading, but they vanish on the stage. And that is the ultimate test of any drama.

Structurally, *The Winter's Tale* is divided into three main parts. The first part runs through Act III, scene ii, and is an almost totally self-contained drama. By itself, it constitutes a Greek tragedy in miniature, ending with Leontes' realization of his tragic error after the deaths of his queen and son. The single unresolved thread of plot that leads to the second part is the casting out of the infant princess by Antigonus; that is the episode (III, iii) with which the second part begins. This central section of the play provides a pastoral interlude in Bohemia and ends at the conclusion of Act

IV. The third part then takes us back to Sicilia for the recovery of the lost princess Perdita and her happy reunion with Leontes and the "resurrected" Hermione. In the progress of this action, sixteen years of dramatic time are presumed to have passed.

Time plays an important role in each of Shakespeare's last four romances; the passage of time serves as a reconstructive or conciliatory influence. In this play especially time is essential in effecting both growth and decay. Time provides the soil that nurtures change, allowing the maturation of Perdita and burying the sorrows caused by Leontes' mad jealousy. The subtitle of the source story by Greene is significant: "The Triumph of Time."

In *Cymbeline* and *The Tempest* time in the story has passed before the play begins; past events are recounted through narrative exposition. In *Pericles* and *The Winter's Tale*, however, the early events of the story are presented on stage, necessitating an interruption in the flow of events. *The Winter's Tale* especially has been criticized for the frankly artificial way in which Shakespeare disposes of sixteen years: the speech, in rhymed couplets, of "Time, as Chorus" at Act IV, scene i:

> I, that please some, try all, both joy and terror
> Of good and bad, that makes and unfolds error,
> Now take upon me, in the name of Time,
> To use my wings. Impute it not a crime
> To me or my swift passage, that I slide
> O'er sixteen years and leave the growth untried
> Of that wide gap.

This major time lapse in the structuring of the plot, although it violates neoclassical ideals of unity, serves a useful purpose in *The Winter's Tale*. It enhances the play's appeal in the theater. How intriguing it is to see both the passionate young Leontes and the older, repentant Leontes; the young Hermione abused, then the mature Hermione serene and triumphant; the dual figures of Paulina, of Camillo, of Polixenes! Much of the theatrical appeal of *The Winter's Tale* would be lost if we were merely to hear recounted in narration the tragic events that constitute the first section of this play. Shakespeare's handling of dramatic time and plot structure here is unconventional—perhaps even "unliterary"—but it makes for first-rate theater.

The tragicomic method of *The Winter's Tale* is quite different from that of *Pericles* and *Cymbeline*. The comic aspect of *Pericles* is minimal and resides almost solely in its happy denouement. The serious and comic elements of *Cymbeline* are fully integrated, occurring simultaneously. In *The Winter's Tale* the tragic action is confined to the first part of the play, while the comic material dominates the second and third parts. The first part of the play is almost unrelievedly solemn, but for the occasional innocent chatter of Mamillius. The tragic tone prevails until Act III, scene iii, a scene that Shakespeare used to good effect in bringing about a transition from the tragic to the comic.

This transitional scene, although set in Bohemia, opens with an extension of the tone and plot of Sicilia: the soliloquy by Antigonus, in which he recounts the visitation of Hermione's ghost. The soliloquy itself signals a shift in tone; its language, unlike the fairly realistic verse of the first part, is fanciful and extravagant. Hermione's ghost, we hear, approached Antigonus "in pure white robes," and, "gasping to begin some speech, her eyes/Became two spouts." After chastising him for casting out the babe, "with shrieks,/She melted into air." The tone of the soliloquy is that of a "winter's tale," spooky and fanciful.

Antigonus' soliloquy is brought to an abrupt conclusion by what is perhaps the most famous stage

direction in Shakespeare: *"Exit, pursued by a bear."*
However much we may pity the fate of poor Antigonus, the visual effect of this exit is undeniably
comic—especially so if the "bear" is an actor in an
animal suit. (Sir Arthur Quiller-Couch suggested that
Shakespeare conceived this exit to take advantage of an
actual trained bear, available from the Bear-Pit in
Southwark, near the Globe Theatre.[2])

The appearance of the bear provides a hilarious
piece of visual comedy, which is then quickly followed
by the appearances of the Shepherd and the Clown—
the former to discover the abandoned princess and the
latter to describe the drowning of the sailors and the
death of Antigonus in the clutches of the bear.
The Clown's description is grotesquely comic as he
tells how the "bear tore out his shoulder-bone" and
how the "poor gentleman roared and the bear mocked
him." Finally the Clown leaves his father to go see "if
the bear be gone from the gentleman and how much
he hath eaten. . . . If there be any of him left, I'll bury
it." By this point Antigonus is no more than a memory,
the audience is laughing heartily, and the gaiety of
Bohemia is upon us.

Once the scene has shifted to Bohemia, the play never
again returns to the tragic tone of the first part, although there are some dark moments in the pastoral
scene (IV, iv). Polixenes' angry denunciation of his
son's love for Perdita and his threat to disinherit the
prince briefly cast a shadow on the jollity of the sheep-
shearing festivity. But for the most part Bohemia is a
happy place. And the final return to Sicilia is even
happier with its joyful reunions and reconciliations.

Although it draws upon the same fanciful story
elements of fictional romance that render *Pericles* and
Cymbeline rather farfetched, *The Winter's Tale* is
surprisingly realistic in many respects. Its language and
versification especially contribute to the effect of

realism. Nearly a third of the dialogue is in prose, and there is no rhyme in the verse passages (the songs and Time's speech excepted). Moreover, the meter of the play's blank verse is unobtrusive; broken lines, incomplete sentences, and involved syntax occur regularly. The people of this play speak as though their minds were at work:

> ARCHIDAMUS. Wherein our entertainment shall shame us we will be justified in our loves; for indeed—
> CAMILLO. Beseech you,—
> ARCHIDAMUS. Verily, I speak it in the freedom of my knowledge: we cannot with such magnificence—in so rare—I know not what to say.
>
> (I, i)

There is realism, too, in Shakespeare's rendering of the Sicilian court. This is no fairy-tale kingdom like those of *Pericles* and *Cymbeline*. There is an emphasis upon domesticity in Leontes' court. Paulina henpecks her husband Antigonus and feels free even to rail at the king if occasion serves (II, iii). Leontes plays with his son and wipes some dirt off his nose (I, ii). Hermione is pestered by her little boy (II, i) but entertains his childish prattle. The Sicilia scenes convey the sense that their characters—Leontes, Camillo, Paulina, Antigonus, Hermione—know and respond to one another as people, not as picture-book kings and queens.

The realistic tone is not, however, confined to Sicilia. The rustic scenes in Bohemia also go beyond the artifice of conventional pastoral romance. The sheepshearing celebration of Act IV, scene iv (the longest single scene in Shakespeare), is not simply the arcadian idyll of so many pastoral romances. It is, rather, a fairly realistic picture of a contemporary Elizabethan festivity. In reference to this scene, E. M. W. Tillyard has written: "Shakespeare never did anything finer, more serious, more evocative of his full powers, than his picture of an earthly paradise painted in the form of the English countryside."[3]

It is true that Florizel and Perdita, in their roles of disguised and undiscovered royalty, respectively, play conventional parts in the sheepshearing scene. But they play against the dominant mood of the festivity—the mood established by the Clown and his two bickering girlfriends Mopsa and Dorcas, by the dancers and musicians, by the old fussbudget Shepherd, and, most importantly, by the roguish Autolycus, confidence man par excellence.

Autolycus (roughly "very wolf") is a true original. Like Jaques in *As You Like It*, he is always there but really does nothing to advance the plot. He recalls Feste (*Twelfth Night*) in his singing, his jesting with the audience, and his freedom from personal ties with the other characters. He bears some kinship with Sir John Falstaff (*Henry IV*) in that he considers lying and cheating to be normal modes of behavior. He is a self-proclaimed rogue and thief:

> My traffic is sheets; when the kite builds, look to lesser linen. My father named me Autolycus; who being, as I am, littered under Mercury, was likewise a snapper-up of unconsidered trifles. With die and drab I purchased this caparison, and my revenue is the silly cheat.
>
> (IV, iii)

He then proceeds to prove his claim by picking the pocket of the dull-witted Clown. This scene provides a delightful opportunity for slapstick; it must be seen to be appreciated.

Autolycus and his low-comedy antics help to counteract the fairy-tale tone of *The Winter's Tale* and emphasize the realistic background before which the other characters play. The last scene (V, ii) with Autolycus, in which he humbles himself before the Shepherd and the Clown, serves as a thematic under-scoring of Leontes' humility in the play's moving final scene. (It has been suggested, in fact, that Shakespeare intended the roguery of Autolycus to be the comic counterpart of the malevolence of Leontes in the tragic action.)

The jealousy of Leontes is probably the least realistic and most purely conventional feature of *The Winter's Tale*. Much has been written of the implausibility with which his jealous suspicions abruptly overtake him, as well as of the tenacity with which he clings to them against all reason. The question of plausibility would not have arisen, however, with the Jacobean audience, who understood well the literary convention of "horn-madness" (irrational fear of being cuckolded).

Leontes has been compared to Othello, but the two are quite different. In *The Winter's Tale* there is no villainous conniver such as Iago to spur the hero to jealousy. Leontes' passion is self-induced and self-sustained. It is to be understood as a sickness—a mad-ness that deprives its victim of the ability to reason. Bertrand Evans called Leontes "Shakespeare's lone example of unqualified self-deception."[4]

Aside from his jealous passion, Leontes is character-ized with consistency and with some degree of realism. He is not a great man, not a story-book king like Cymbeline. He behaves more like a husband and father than a ruler, and he shows human failings by his im-maturity, bad temper, and feelings of persecution. Despite his irrational behavior in the first part of the play, Leontes is normally well liked by his courtiers. Camillo is a faithful friend to him and prefers to flee rather than acquiesce to his temporary madness. Paulina's seeming shrewishness is motivated by a fer-vent desire to bring her sovereign and friend back to his senses, and in the latter part of the play she is still affectionately (if a trifle naggingly) ministering to him. Hermione, in the face of Leontes' outrageous accusations and cruelty to her, never once abandons her love for him.

The reappearance of Hermione in the play's final scene is one of the most amazing bits of theatrical legerdemain in Shakespeare. Whatever its implausibility at the level of realism, it creates a stunning effect in the playing and provides a supreme moment of wonder and spirituality to which no audience can fail to respond.

There is no similar instance in Shakespeare's plays of an audience's expectations being deliberately led astray—no other event so devoid of preparation or foreshadowing. (In *Much Ado about Nothing*, Hero is said to have died after the altar scene, but the audience knows that she is alive. Not so with Hermione.) It is not simply that the audience is allowed to believe Hermione dead; we are repeatedly made to believe it.

Paulina tearfully and convincingly reports Hermione's death in Act III, scene ii, immediately after the queen has swooned and been carried from the courtroom. When the First Lord expresses incredulity, Paulina responds: "I say she's dead: I'll swear't. If word nor oath/Prevail not, go and see." At the close of the scene Leontes exits, presumably to view the body: "Prithee, bring me/To the dead bodies of my queen and son:/One grave shall be for both." In the very next scene Antigonus recounts the visitation of Hermione's ghost. Every reference to Hermione gives positive assurance that she has indeed died.

It is not until the first scene of Act V that a few hints of Hermione's survival begin to surface. Paulina has exacted from Leontes a promise never to remarry "unless another,/As like Hermione as is her picture,/Affront his eye." If he is to remarry, states Paulina, his new bride "shall be such/As, walk'd your first queen's ghost, it should take joy/To see her in your arms." In the following scene the Third Gentleman speaks of the statue of the dead queen, sculpted by Julio Romano who "so near to Hermione hath done Hermione that they say one would speak to her and stand in hope of answer." The Second Gentleman then tells of Paulina's daily visits over the past sixteen years to the house where the statue is kept. By this point the spectator may begin to suspect that some unusual and significant event will center on this mysterious statue.

It is not until the statue is revealed, however, that the audience knows that Hermione lives. There is no stagecraft that can make us believe we behold a statue, once the actress playing Hermione is revealed. All those on stage (except, of course, Paulina and Hermione herself) are deceived, but we are not. And that is precisely Shakespeare's intention. His management of theatrical effect here is masterful. From the moment the curtain is drawn aside until Hermione steps down from her pedestal, some eighty lines of dialogue are spoken—approximately four or five minutes of playing time. This is the time during which the audience, now at last superior in knowledge to the characters, anticipates the "resurrection" of Hermione and the reconciliation that must surely follow. It is an interval of pure suspense, during which the dramatic tension builds. Had we known all along of Hermione's preservation, the emotional effect of this moment would be dissipated. Shakespeare has concentrated and intensified our anticipation of Hermione's rebirth. When it finally comes, to the accompaniment of solemn music, so comes our joy; the tears fall freely. No one who has experienced this moment in the theater can question its affective power, its spirituality, and its supreme joy.

The reunion of Hermione and Leontes, too profoundly moving for words, is effected in a silent embrace; her single speech is to her daughter Perdita:

> You gods, look down
> And from your sacred vials pour your graces
> Upon my daughter's head! Tell me, mine own,
> Where hast thou been preserved? where lived?
> how found
> Thy father's court? for thou shalt hear that I,
> Knowing by Paulina that the oracle
> Gave hope thou wast in being, have preserved
> Myself to see the issue.

In this final scene Shakespeare's principal theme—reconcilement—is made manifest in the most moving of actions. It is a theme that is stated also in *Pericles* and *Cymbeline*, but not so powerfully or affectingly as in *The Winter's Tale*. Through the healing ministration of "this great gap of time," "that which is lost [is] found," past sins are forgiven and sorrows forgotten, and we are shown a world redeemed—a world "in which the sins of the fathers are not visited on the children."[5]

The stage history of *The Winter's Tale* is somewhat spotty. The play was evidently quite popular during the reigns of James I and Charles I, with several performances being recorded through 1640. Then the play disappeared from theatrical records for a hundred years.

In 1741 *The Winter's Tale* was revived at the Goodman's Fields theater in London, in the equivalent of what would be called today an off-Broadway production. Then came the inevitable eighteenth-century alterations, of which two are noteworthy. The first version was called *The Sheep-Shearing; or, Florizel and Perdita* (1754). It was joined two years later by David Garrick's *Florizel and Perdita*. Both versions

Autolycus the rogue (Daniel Davis, center) confronts the old Shepherd (Sydney Walker) and his son the Clown (Thomas M. Nahrwold) in the American Conservatory Theater (San Francisco) production of *The Winter's Tale*, 1978.

WILLIAM GANSLEN

were played repeatedly through the remainder of the century, and it is often difficult to know from the records which was which, due to the similarity of their titles.

In 1802 John Philip Kemble produced *The Winter's Tale* at the Drury Lane Theatre in a version close to Shakespeare's original, with the great Sarah Siddons as Hermione. Subsequent nineteenth-century productions included those by Charles Macready (1823), Samuel Phelps (1845), and Edmund Kean (1856), the last being notable for its attempt to reproduce with complete historical accuracy the costumes and decor of ancient Greece.

One particularly notable nineteenth-century production of *The Winter's Tale* was that by Mary Anderson at London's Lyceum Theatre in 1887. Miss Anderson herself played both Hermione and Perdita (!) with great success. Johnston Forbes-Robertson was Leontes.

Twentieth-century productions of note have included those of Herbert Beerbohm Tree (1906), Harley Granville-Barker (1912), and Peter Brook (1951). Tree had the great Ellen Terry for his Hermione, but did not himself take a role. Granville-Barker's production at the Savoy represented a breakthrough in Shakespearean stage production. He mounted the play on a platform stage, without scenery, and played the action continuously, with but one intermission—a unique and controversial approach at that time. Brook's version was notable for its stellar cast, which included John Gielgud as Leontes, Diana Wynyard as Hermione, and Flora Robson as Paulina.

The Winter's Tale, although not frequently produced on the contemporary stage, is a work that never fails to please. It is theatrical in the best sense of the word—rich in character and conflict, needing the magic of the theater for its fullest realization.

The Tempest

The Tempest is generally regarded as Shake-speare's crowning achievement in comedy. Written in 1610 or 1611, it is the last of his comic works (virtually his last drama, since *Henry VIII*, the final play in the Shakespeare canon, is a collaboration). Critics agree that this play is a dramatic masterpiece, but they differ widely in their reasons for believing it to be so. *The Tempest* is possibly Shakespeare's most interpreted comedy.

Among the more persuasive of interpretations have been those that find in the play some allegorical system. One such theory, for example, sees *The Tempest* as a pastoral allegory. Prospero represents Art, in opposition to Caliban as Nature. Caliban is a representation of Natural Man, "like the shepherd in formal pastoral."[1] Another possibility is that Ariel and Caliban represent disparate aspects of the human condition—the spiritual and the corporeal. Ariel and Caliban have also been interpreted as facets of Prospero's personality.

But the interpretation that has gained most attention in this century is the one that sees Prospero as Shake-speare himself, consciously embodying in *The Tempest* an autobiographical account of his career as well as his personal farewell to the stage. The theory is too complex for full discussion here, but its proponents point out that Prospero is an imaginative and creative being who deals in magic and illusions, transforming the real world, as does the dramatist. It is Shakespeare talking, these critics say, when Prospero resigns his magic (the theater?):

> But this rough magic
> I here abjure, and, when I have required
> Some heavenly music,
> . . . .
> I'll break my staff,
> Bury it certain fathoms in the earth,
> And deeper than did ever plummet sound
> I'll drown my book.
>
> (V, i)

In the play's epilogue, spoken by Prospero, these same interpreters hear Shakespeare making his apology before his audience as he indicates his intention to retire to his home in Stratford.

This autobiographical interpretation of *The Tempest* is by no means universally accepted, however. A most effective spokesman for the opposition was E. E. Stoll:

> I cannot believe that there is any allegory . . . or symbolism . . . or even "veiled biography" here. . . . And Prospero is not Shakespeare; . . . his "potent art" of magic is not the art of poetry; Ariel is not genius, or the lawless imagination, craving liberty but kept in service; Miranda is not the drama; Caliban not the vulgar public; Milan not Stratford; and the enchanted isle not the stage, or London, or the world.[2]

Stoll's rejection of the autobiographical interpretation was seconded by T. M. Parrott, who found it "incredible that a practical playwright, composing, at the very end of his career, a play for Blackfriars and the Court, should consciously turn it into an allegory of his art or a cryptic version of the soul's aspiration."[3]

Perhaps the commentators have been so eager to interpret the play because of its deceptive simplicity; surely so clear and accessible a work must have some deeper meaning? For Shakespeare tells his story in *The Tempest* with great economy, perfect clarity, and rigorous adherence to the famed Three Unities of dramatic construction so precious to the neoclassicists. Only in his first comedy, *The Comedy of Errors*, did Shakespeare come close to achieving the neoclassical unity found in *The Tempest*.

This unity is achieved primarily through Shakespeare's treatment of time. Like the stories told in *Pericles* and *The Winter's Tale*, that of *The Tempest* involves a considerable span of time. In those earlier works, however, the passage of time is structured into the plot. Fourteen years pass during the course of *Pericles*, sixteen during *The Winter's Tale*. By contrast, in *The Tempest* Shakespeare chose as his point of attack the very day on which the story reaches its crisis. The entire earlier tale—Antonio's usurpation of Prospero's dukedom and the casting away of Prospero and Miranda—is narrated by Prospero (I, ii) and quickly disposed of.

Thus, *The Tempest* observes perfect Unity of Time, Place, and Action. Prospero tells us in Act I, scene ii, that the time of day is two o'clock; in the final scene we learn that it is six o'clock. Since the entire action occurs on the enchanted island (the opening tempest excepted), Unity of Place is observed. And the emphasis upon Prospero as protagonist precludes subplots or divided focus, thus providing Unity of Action.

This classical approach to dramatic structure gives *The Tempest* an extraordinary compactness and clarity of story line, allowing the play to make its effect swiftly and intensively. It also robs the comedy of much of the variety and copiousness of intrigue so characteristic of Shakespeare's other comedies. Compared to *Cymbeline*, a play it much resembles in scope and theme, *The Tempest* appears almost static and devoid of intrigue.

There are, of course, some plot intrigues in *The Tempest*. Prospero engineers the union of Miranda and Ferdinand by pretending to disapprove of their romance, testing the youth with the task of the log-carrying, "lest too light winning/Make the prize light" (I, ii). Antonio and Sebastian plot the assassination of Alonso (II, i), and the comical trio of Caliban, Trinculo, and Stephano mount a similar campaign against Prospero (III, ii). Nevertheless, the intrigues of *The Tempest* are artificial—trumped up—and never truly menacing.

This is so, of course, because of the character of Prospero, the omnipotent, omniscient, and even prescient stage manager of the play's action. No other Shakespeare character is possessed of such complete control over the play in which he figures. The closest approximation is Oberon (*A Midsummer Night's Dream*), but even Oberon is victimized by the mischievous ineptitude of his chief lieutenant Puck. Ariel, *The Tempest*'s analogue to Puck, is infallible and nearly as powerful as his master.

Since we know from the outset that all is in Prospero's control—indeed, has been carefully arranged by him—we can never experience the apprehension and suspense that Shakespeare's intrigues normally create. This makes for a singular lack of dramatic tension throughout *The Tempest*. As many commentators have pointed out, very little actually happens in the play. It has no central conflict.

The play's brief opening scene is perhaps its most

suspenseful and exciting one, occurring as it does before we know of Prospero's existence. In it, we witness a storm-tossed ship on perilous seas. A king is among the men aboard, all of whom will surely drown. It is the most tumultuous opening scene in Shakespeare, but it is followed by one of the most static scenes in Shakespeare. Prospero immediately puts our fear (and Miranda's) to rest by assuring us that the calamity we have just witnessed is an illusion: "No more amazement: tell your piteous heart/There's no harm done. . . . No harm" (I, ii).

This comforting assurance is followed by the most protracted passage of exposition in all of Shakespeare. Prospero sits his daughter down and narrates to her (and to us) the entire background of the play. So artificially is this exposition contrived that the story-teller must repeatedly demand the listener's (ours as well as Miranda's) attention:

> I pray thee, mark me. . . . Dost thou attend
>   me? . . .
> Thou attend'st not. . . . I pray thee, mark
>   me. . . .
> Dost thou hear? . . . Hear a little further
> And then I'll bring thee to the present business
> Which now's upon 's; without the which this
>   story
> Were most impertinent.

Impertinent, indeed! But absolutely necessary in order that the dramatist can provide his audience with full knowledge of past events and get on with the present action. This expository scene is the result of *The Tempest*'s neoclassical structure, and it contributes greatly to the play's climate of stasis.

We learn almost from the first, then, that Prospero is in control of all the shipwrecked Italians. Thanks to Ariel, his ubiquitous "eyes," no act can escape his vision. Ariel himself creates the opportunity for the assassination plot (II, i) by putting the intended victim, Alonso, and his attendants to sleep. Thus, we view the villainous scheming as a deliberate plan by Ariel and can experience no real fear for the life of the king. And in answer to our expectations, Ariel reappears just at the critical moment to awaken the sleepers and abort the coup.

The plot against Prospero is similarly defused. We can never for a moment believe that any practice against this omniscient mage could succeed, let alone one concocted by such bunglers as the drunken Stephano and the idiotic Trinculo (III, ii). Their resolve to kill Prospero is little more to us than comic relief, conceived as it is in foolery and slapstick. Ariel's overseeing of their plotting removes any potential for harm; he tells us that he will inform Prospero of the plot. When the fourth-act masque captures our attention, we completely forget the scheming trio. Prospero himself, interrupting the masque, must remind us that this thread of dramatic intrigue is still unresolved:

> I had forgot that foul conspiracy
> Of the beast Caliban and his confederates
> Against my life: the minute of their plot
> Is almost come. (*To the Spirits.*) Well done!
>   avoid; no more!

The little suspense generated by the abortive plot against Prospero stems from our curiosity over his intended method of stopping it. The suspense is dissipated a mere fifty lines later, when the conspirators are easily dissuaded from their treachery by the "glistering apparel" that Ariel places before them. The conspirators are suitably punished, in the comic mode —drenched in the "filthy-mantled pool" and driven from the stage by "*divers Spirits, in shape of dogs and hounds.*" Even Caliban, formerly the most recalcitrant of slaves, learns his lesson:

> I'll be wise heareafter
> And seek for grace. What a thrice-double ass
> Was I, to take this drunkard [Stephano] for a
>   god
> And worship this dull fool!
>
>   (V, i)

Conspiracy, then, provides the single note of intrigue in *The Tempest.* The three comic conspirators, in addition to providing the only low-comedy action in the play, offer a parodic version of the larger intrigue: the political treachery of the Italian nobles, both past and present. Caliban's enlistment of Stephano as his coconspirator against his master Prospero parodies Antonio's action in recruiting Sebastian's aid in the attempt on Alonso. The usurpation of authority by unworthy pretenders is the theme of both actions, and both intrigues are foiled by Prospero's omnipotence.

The more serious conspiracy, that of Antonio and Sebastian against Alonso, seems in the reading a rather pointless affair, being quickly foiled by Ariel's intervention at the moment of its inception. But its inclusion in the play is a masterful touch. This brief incident of treachery serves as an effective device for recalling, on the stage, the original treacherous act that set the entire story in motion: Antonio's usurpation, twelve years earlier, of Prospero's rightful dukedom in Milan. This crucial act from the past, given to us only in Prospero's long narrative (I, ii), is reinforced—in a sense dramatically recreated—in the present. As always, Shakespeare knew how to maximize the theatricality of his narrative material.

The Tempest is clearly the most theatrical of Shakespeare's comedies—the one that most consistently draws upon the resources of the theater and exploits them for entertainment value. This is obvious in its music and sound effects, in its elaborate stage directions and magic tricks, and in its utilization of the Jacobean court masque.

The play is filled with music, both vocal and instrumental. Ariel sings repeatedly; Juno and Ceres vocalize in the wedding masque; even the drunken Stephano is given a ribald chantey to sing. Ariel's magic spells are accompanied by "*solemn and strange music*." Caliban tells his mates that the "isle is full of noises":

> Sounds and sweet airs, that give delight and
>   hurt not.
> Sometimes a thousand twangling instruments
> Will hum about mine ears, and sometime voices
> That, if I then had waked after long sleep,
> Will make me sleep again.
>
> (III, ii)

Nonmusical sounds also abound on this enchanted isle. The stage directions indicate them in some detail: "*a tempestuous noise of thunder and lightning heard*," "*a confused noise within*," "*a noise of thunder heard*," "*a strange, hollow, and confused noise*," "*a noise of hunters heard*," and so on.

Stage effects are far more extensive in *The Tempest* than in any other Shakespeare play, indicating that the work was intended for indoor presentation, in a theater equipped to handle such effects. The opening storm establishes this theatrical mode and provides opportunities for some rather spectacular staging. For example, in the 1979 production at the Mark Taper Forum of the Los Angeles Music Center, at the conclusion of the storm scene the scenic drop representing the ship, together with its accompanying ground-cloth, was literally sucked down into a large hole in the stage floor, revealing the enchanted isle behind— a stunning scenic effect.

In addition to the tempest itself, we are treated to other visual effects in this comedy. Actors appear costumed as *"strange Shapes,"* classical goddesses, dogs and hounds. Ariel, no ordinary creature in his normal dress, appears as a harpy (III, iii). And Caliban, the grotesque "moon-calf," presents a classic challenge to an imaginative costumer. A banquet is presented to the stranded Italians (III, iii) and is then made to vanish *"with a quaint device."* We are shown the literal hounding of the comic trio; a dance of Reapers and Nymphs; and, of course, the wedding masque itself, with all its theatrical splendor.

The Tempest owes much to the Jacobean court masque, an elaborate theatrical entertainment popular in the early seventeenth century. Shakespeare had included masquelike elements in earlier plays (for example, *Love's Labor's Lost*, *A Midsummer Night's Dream*, and *As You Like It*), but never a masque with the prominence of that in *The Tempest*. Since the occasion of the masque is the betrothal of Ferdinand and Miranda, it accordingly celebrates fertility. Iris, goddess of the rainbow and messenger of the gods, serves as "presenter," calling forth Ceres, goddess of abundance, and Juno, the wife of great Jupiter himself. The goddesses converse and sing, assuring fertility and abundance. The masque ends with a dance as Prospero, remembering the plot against him, stops the performance and sends the masquers away. The entire scene is, as Ferdinand terms it, a "most majestic vision, and/ Harmonious charmingly," and Prospero's epilogue to the masque contains the play's finest passage of poetry:

> Our revels now are ended. These our actors,
> As I foretold you, were all spirits and

Are melted into air, into thin air:
And, like the baseless fabric of this vision,
The cloud-capp'd towers, the gorgeous palaces,
The solemn temples, the great globe itself,
Yea, all which it inherit, shall dissolve
And, like this insubstantial pageant faded,
Leave not a rack behind. We are such stuff
As dreams are made on, and our little life
Is rounded with a sleep.

Ferdinand and Miranda, the couple in whose honor the masque is celebrated, are the finest of the idealized young couples that populate Shakespeare's last four romances. Ferdinand epitomizes devotion and honor as he performs the love-labor of the log-carrying and vows to Prospero that nothing "shall ever melt/Mine honour into lust" (IV, i) where Miranda is concerned. Miranda is perfect obedience and beauty, wide-eyed with wonder at beholding the first man (apart from her father) that she has ever seen. Ferdinand is to her a "thing divine, for nothing natural/I ever saw so noble" (I, ii).

Prospero's pretended anger at the love between his daughter and the young prince recalls the similar stratagem of old Simonides (*Pericles*), who brought together his daughter Thaisa and Pericles by feigning displeasure at their mutual attraction. There is a parallel here also to the anger of Polixenes (*The Winter's Tale*) upon learning that his son Prince Florizel loves the shepherdess Perdita. However, Polixenes' wrath creates dramatic tension, since we know that it is genuine. Prospero's ruse serves little dramatic purpose, creating rather the illusion of conflict than the genuine article.

The issue of the heroine's chastity is less prominent in *The Tempest* than in the other three romances. Caliban's servitude (and by implication his ugliness) results from his past attempt to rape Miranda, but no test is made of her virtue within the play itself—again, an indication of this comedy's singular lack of dramatic conflict. Ferdinand is explicit in his determination to honor her virginity. Indeed, it is Prospero who suggests that it could be otherwise, and Ferdinand is indignant at the suggestion. When the betrothed couple is presented to the newly reconciled noblemen in the final scene, the lovers are revealed in tableau, playing at a game of chess. Here is achieved in visual symbolism the happy union of physical passion with reason. (Chess was also an activity conventionally associated with high-born and romantic lovers.)

Aside from Miranda the only other regular residents of *The Tempest*'s enchanted isle are Ariel, Caliban, and Prospero. Their relationship is one of interdependency, the mortal being master of both earthbound beast and airy spirit. In order to function, Prospero depends not only upon the swift servitude of Ariel but also upon the grudging labors of Caliban, who "does make our fire,/Fetch in our wood and serves in offices/That profit us" (I, ii).

Caliban (anagram for "cannibal," a general term for a Caribbean savage) helps to humanize Prospero's characterization; the magician's attitude toward the rebellious slave is that of a parent toward a wayward child. Caliban's actual parents were a devil and a witch; small wonder he should be so foul! Prospero calls him

> A devil, a born devil, on whose nature
> Nurture can never stick; on whom my pains,
> Humanely taken, all, all lost, quite lost;
> And as with age his body uglier grows,
> So his mind cankers.
>
> (IV, i)

But this ugly "devil" does profit from Prospero's pains, coming to realize that he will fare better by serving his master obediently than by following the false "god" Stephano. Even after Caliban's treachery against him is exposed, Prospero will not disown the "misshapen knave." To the others he confesses: "This thing of darkness I/Acknowledge mine" (V, i).

Ariel is the converse of Caliban—all lightness, air, and obedience. By obeying his master's commands to the letter he finally gains his freedom, whereas Caliban remains in servitude. The characterization of Ariel is the most tenuous in the play. He exists chiefly on the symbolic level and really has no distinctive personality, assuming at any given moment the identity that Prospero requires of him: singer, hypnotist, harpy, Master of Revels, and so on. Ariel is essentially a device of the plot. The character is perhaps the most difficult in Shakespeare to represent successfully on the stage. (The role, incidentally, is frequently played by a woman.)

In the characterization of Prospero, Shakespeare went beyond the semisymbolic royal figures of the earlier romances, combining the human with the divine. In his role of omnipotent manipulator of the others' fates, Prospero is an elaborated version of those deities who function briefly in the other romances—the Diana of *Pericles*, the Jupiter of *Cymbeline*, and the unseen but influential Apollo of *The Winter's Tale*. Unlike those deities, however, Prospero is a feeling man with human qualities. His paternal tenderness is obvious. He is also subject to anger and even forgetfulness (IV, i). His magical power, too, is "humanized"; the craft of a scholar or scientist, it derives from books and study. In Prospero, Shakespeare achieved the remarkable feat of creating a magician with supernatural powers who never seems less than fully human.

The Tempest offers a restatement of the story elements and themes that appear in the three earlier romances. As in those plays we have a tale of lost royalty, of adventures by sea (the sea once again an instrument of Fortune), of parents and children, and of the ultimate recovery of the lost royalty. *The Tempest* even provides the "resurrection" of a royal personage presumed dead (Ferdinand), a reminder of Thaisa, Imogen, and Hermione.

It is in its recapitulation of the thematic content of the earlier romances, however, that *The Tempest* excels. This comedy most successfully dramatizes the happy emergence into a new and better world of the children of former enemies, together with the marital union of those children. Past treacheries between royal persons are nullified through the ministrations of time, and former enemies are at last reconciled. These themes were essayed in the earlier plays.

In none of the other romances, however, was the emphasis placed so strongly upon the virtue of forgiveness. Prospero, a prince greatly wronged, has a unique opportunity for revenge. His former enemies are at his mercy and have amply demonstrated the malice that still reigns in their hearts. But Prospero must rise above the lust for vengeance:

> Though with their high wrongs I am struck to
>   the quick,
> Yet with my nobler reason gainst my fury
> Do I take part: the rarer action is
> In virtue than in vengeance: they being
>   penitent,
> The sole drift of my purpose doth extend
> Not a frown further.
>
> (V, i)

When Alonso, Sebastian, and Antonio stand charmed and motionless before him, Prospero bestows his forgiveness upon the evildoers. And as if through the medicinal power of charity and forgiveness, the offen-

The inhabitants of *The Tempest*'s enchanted isle: Miranda (Stephanie Zimbalist), Ariel (Brent Carver), Prospero (Anthony Hopkins), and Caliban (Michael Bond, below). From the Center Theatre Group/Mark Taper Forum (Los Angeles) production in 1979 (Gordon Davidson, Artistic Director). Directed by John Hirsch; set design by Ming Cho Lee; costume design by Carrie F. Robbins.

JAY THOMPSON

ders are dramatically transformed. Miranda, viewing the company for the first time, must exclaim:

> O, wonder!
> How many goodly creatures are there here!
> How beauteous mankind is! O brave new
>   world,
> That has such people in 't!

For all its ready theatricality, *The Tempest* is, strangely, one Shakespeare comedy that seems to please more in the reading than in the enactment. Much of the beauty of the play resides in its language. Its poetry is powerfully evocative and conjures up images that may not always be successfully conveyed in the literalness of stage presentation.

What actor, for example, can ever achieve in the role of Ariel the lightness, swiftness, and instantaneous appearances and disappearances suggested by the text? When he exits with the words "I drink the air before me, and return/Or ere your pulse twice beat" (V, i), the line serves only to call attention to the earthbound body of the actor. Such an exit can be viewed only in the mind's eye. Similarly, no amount of ingenuity on the part of the costumer can match the grotesqueness of Caliban as he is described in poetic images. In fact, the more elaborate the costume the more our admiration shifts from Shakespeare's Caliban to the costumer's Caliban.

Nevertheless, *The Tempest* has enjoyed a successful stage history and is among the more frequently produced of Shakespeare's comedies. Throughout the seventeenth and eighteenth centuries Shakespeare's original text was largely ignored in favor of various operatic adaptations, the most popular being *The Tempest; or, The Enchanted Isle* by William Davenant and John Dryden, first played in 1667. Shakespeare's *The Tempest* gradually reemerged in the next century, receiving notable productions by William Charles Macready in 1838, Samuel Phelps in 1847 and 1849, and Herbert Beerbohm Tree in 1904.

In our own century, *The Tempest* has almost always been played in its original version, and the operatic "improvements" have slipped into a well-deserved oblivion. Walter Hampden made a noteworthy Prospero in 1916, as did Arnold Moss in Margaret Webster's 1945 production.

Perhaps the most stellar cast assembled for *The Tempest* in recent years was that of the 1955 production at Stratford, Connecticut. Raymond Massey was Prospero, backed by Joan Chandler as Miranda, Jack Palance as Caliban, Roddy McDowell as Ariel, and Christopher Plummer as Ferdinand. *The Tempest* has always appealed to actors. Ariel and Caliban provide opportunities for flamboyant character performances, and Prospero is one of the great Shakespearean roles.

NOTES

The Comedy of Errors

1. *The Complete Works of Shakespeare*, ed. Hardin Craig (Chicago, Scott, Foresman, 1961), pp. 81–82.
2. Spelling, punctuation, and precise wording in Shakespeare's plays will vary slightly from one edition to another. The quotations of Shakespeare in this volume are taken from Hardin Craig's edition of *The Complete Works of Shakespeare*.

The Taming of the Shrew

1. *Shakespeare: The Complete Works*, ed. G. B. Harrison (New York, Harcourt, Brace & World, 1948), p. 332.
2. *The Complete Works of Shakespeare*, ed. Hardin Craig, p. 154.
3. At least one of Shakespeare's contemporaries evidently felt that Petruchio was a bully who deserved his "comeuppance." John Fletcher wrote a sequel to *The Taming of the Shrew*, called *The Woman's Prize; or, The Tamer Tamed* (ca. 1625), in which Petruchio,

after the death of Katharine, marries an aggressive woman who breaks *his* spirit and tames *him*.

The Two Gentlemen of Verona

1. H. B. Charlton, *Shakespearian Comedy* (New York, Barnes & Noble, 1961), p. 41.

Love's Labor's Lost

1. John Dover Wilson, *Shakespeare's Happy Comedies* (Evanston, Ill., Northwestern University Press, 1962), p. 65.
2. *Shakespeare: The Complete Works*, ed. G. B. Harrison (New York, Harcourt, Brace & World, 1948), p. 394.
3. C. L. Barber, *Shakespeare's Festive Comedy* (Princeton, N.J., Princeton University Press, 1959), p. 93.
4. Harley Granville-Barker, *Prefaces to Shakespeare*, (Princeton, N.J., Princeton University Press, 1963), vol. 4, p. 5.
5. Wilson, *Shakespeare's Happy Comedies*, p. 66.

A Midsummer Night's Dream

1. Ralph Berry, *Shakespeare's Comedies* (Princeton, N.J., Princeton University Press, 1972), pp. 95–96.

The Merchant of Venice

1. Charlton, *Shakespearian Comedy*, p. 128.
2. Wilson, *Shakespeare's Happy Comedies*, p. 105.
3. Charlton, *Shakespearian Comedy*, pp. 127–30.
4. Barber, *Shakespeare's Festive Comedy*, p. 179.
5. Frank Kermode, *Shakespeare, Spenser, Donne* (New York, The Viking Press, 1971), p. 214.

6. *The Merchant of Venice*, ed. Sir Arthur Quiller-Couch, Cambridge Shakespeare (Cambridge, The University Press, 1953), p. xxxi.

The Merry Wives of Windsor

1. Bertrand Evans saw the unexpected appearance of Mistress Quickly as Queen of the Fairies as a deliberate move on Shakespeare's part. Evans theorized that the dramatist substituted "that sly old schemer, ubiquitous busybody, double and triple dealer" for Anne Page as a veiled insult to Queen Elizabeth. The audience could hardly have failed to appreciate the allusion in a Fairy Queen of Windsor Park, and Shakespeare was expressing his distaste at being commanded to create an amorous Falstaff. (*Shakespeare's Comedies* [Oxford, The Clarendon Press, 1960], p. 117.)
2. Charlton, *Shakespearian Comedy*, p. 193.
3. Wilson, *Shakespeare's Happy Comedies*, p. 88.
4. Charlton, *Shakespearian Comedy*, pp. 193–97.
5. Berry, *Shakespeare's Comedies*, pp. 146–53.

Much Ado about Nothing

1. The following piece of dialogue from this same scene (II, iii) provides additional evidence of Shakespeare's intention to pun on "noting":

> Don Pedro.   Now, pray thee, come;
>   Or, if thou wilt hold longer argument,
>   Do it in notes.
> Balthasar.   Note this before my notes;
>   There's not a note of mine that's worth the
>   noting.
>
> Don Pedro. Why, these are very crotchets that he
>   speaks;
>   Note, notes, forsooth, and nothing.

As You Like It

1. It is generally thought that Shakespeare created this new type of witty fool to suit the talents of Robert Armin, a comedian who joined Shakespeare's company, the Lord Chamberlain's Men, at this time.
2. Quoted in *As You Like It*, ed. Agnes Latham, Arden Shakespeare (London, Methuen, 1975), p. xci.

Twelfth Night

1. Berry, *Shakespeare's Comedies*, p. 196.

Troilus and Cressida

1. E. K. Chambers, "Shakespeare: An Epilogue," *Review of English Studies*, 16 (1940):400.
2. Oscar James Campbell, *Shakespeare's Satire* (Hamden, Conn., Archon, 1963), p. 98.
3. *Troilus and Cressida*, ed. Alice Walker, Cambridge Shakespeare (Cambridge, The University Press, 1957), p. xviii.
4. *Troilus and Cressida*, ed. Joseph Papp, The Festival Shakespeare (New York, The Macmillan Company, 1967), p. 23.

All's Well That Ends Well

1. Charlton, *Shakespearian Comedy*, p. 217.
2. William Witherle Lawrence, *Shakespeare's Problem Comedies* (New York, Frederick Ungar, new ed., 1960), p. 61.
3. From Johnson's *Notes* to his 1765 edition of Shakespeare; quoted in Lawrence, *Problem Comedies*, p. 35.
4. Charlton, *Shakespearian Comedy*, p. 217.
5. E. M. W. Tillyard, *Shakespeare's Problem Plays*

(Toronto, University of Toronto Press, 1950), p. 106.
6. George Bernard Shaw, *Our Theatres in the Nineties*
(London, Constable, 1931), Vol. I, p. 30.

Measure for Measure

1. Kenneth Tynan, *He That Plays the King* (London,
Longmans, Green, 1950), p. 151.

Pericles, Prince of Tyre

1. Evans, *Shakespeare's Comedies*, p. 237.

Cymbeline

1. Granville-Barker, *Prefaces to Shakespeare*, vol. 2,
p. 128.
2. *Cymbeline*, ed. J. M. Nosworthy, Arden Shakespeare (London, Methuen, 1955), p. liii.
3. M. R. Ridley, *Shakespeare's Plays: A Commentary*
(London, J. M. Dent, 1937), p. 205.
4. From Swinburne's *Study of Shakespeare* (1879);
quoted in *Cymbeline*, ed. J. C. Maxwell, Cambridge
Shakespeare (Cambridge, The University Press, 1960),
p. xxviii.

The Winter's Tale

1. *The Winter's Tale*, ed. J. H. P. Pafford, Arden
Shakespeare (London, Methuen, 1963), p. xxxviii.
2. *The Winter's Tale*, ed. Sir Arthur Quiller-Couch,
Cambridge Shakespeare (Cambridge, The University
Press, 1959), p. xx.
3. E. M. W. Tillyard, *Shakespeare's Last Plays* (London, Chatto and Windus, 1968), p. 43.

4. Evans, *Shakespeare's Comedies*, p. 291.

5. *Winter's Tale*, Quiller-Couch, Cambridge ed., p. xix.

The Tempest

1. *The Tempest*, ed. Frank Kermode, Arden Shakespeare, 6th ed. (Cambridge, Mass., Harvard University Press, 1958), p. xxiv.

2. As quoted in *Twentieth Century Interpretations of "The Tempest,"* ed. Hallett Smith (Englewood Cliffs, N.J., Prentice-Hall, 1969), p. 25.

3. Thomas Marc Parrott, *Shakespearean Comedy* (New York, Russell & Russell, 1962), p. 395.

BIBLIOGRAPHY

1. Selected Editions of Shakespeare

MULTI-VOLUME EDITIONS

Ellis-Fermor, Una, Harold F. Brooks, Harold Jenkins, et al., eds., *The Arden Shakespeare*, London, Methuen, 1951–present. The Arden Shakespeare devotes a single volume to each play. Introductory material is particularly valuable, as are the extensive notes to the texts.

Furness, H. H., et al., eds., *A New Variorum Edition of Shakespeare*, Philadelphia, Lippincott (and successors), 1871–present. The *Variorum* editions of Shakespeare's plays (one volume per play) offer the most complete critical and textual treatments of all editions, including selections from Shakespeare's plot sources and much historical criticism.

Quiller-Couch, Sir Arthur, and John Dover Wilson, eds., *The Works of Shakespeare*, Cambridge, The University Press, 1948–present. The New Cambridge editions of Shakespeare's plays offer scholarly introductions, extensive notes, and brief stage histories of each play.

ONE-VOLUME EDITIONS

Craig, Hardin, ed., *The Complete Works of Shakespeare*, Chicago, Scott, Foresman, 1961.

Harbage, Alfred, general editor, *William Shakespeare: The Complete Works*, Baltimore, Penguin Books, 1969.

Harrison, G. B., ed., *Shakespeare: The Complete Works*, New York, Harcourt, Brace & World, 1948.

2. Critical Works on Shakespeare's Comedies

Barber, C. L., *Shakespeare's Festive Comedy*, Princeton, N.J., Princeton University Press, 1959.

Barnet, Sylvan, ed., *Twentieth Century Interpretations of "The Merchant of Venice,"* Englewood Cliffs, N.J., Prentice-Hall, 1970.

Berry, Ralph, *Shakespeare's Comedies*, Princeton, N.J., Princeton University Press, 1972.

Campbell, Oscar James, *Shakespeare's Satire*, Hamden, Conn., Archon Books, 1963.

Charlton, H. B., *Shakespearian Comedy*, New York, Barnes & Noble, 1961.

Davis, Walter R., ed., *Twentieth Century Interpretations of "Much Ado about Nothing,"* Englewood Cliffs, N.J., Prentice-Hall, 1969.

Evans, Bertrand, *Shakespeare's Comedies*, Oxford, The Clarendon Press, 1960.

Foakes, R. A., *Shakespeare: The Dark Comedies to the Last Plays*, Charlottesville, University Press of Virginia, 1971.

Geckle, George L., ed., *Twentieth Century Interpretations of "Measure for Measure,"* Englewood Cliffs, N.J., Prentice-Hall, 1970.

Granville-Barker, Harley, *More Prefaces to Shakespeare*, Princeton, N.J., Princeton University Press, 1974.

————, *Prefaces to Shakespeare*, 4 vols., Princeton, N.J., Princeton University Press, 1963.

Halio, Jay L., ed., *Twentieth Century Interpretations of "As You Like It,"* Englewood Cliffs, N.J., Prentice-Hall, 1968.

Harbage, Alfred, *William Shakespeare: A Reader's Guide*, New York, Farrar, Straus, & Giroux, 1963.

Hartwig, Joan, *Shakespeare's Tragicomic Vision*, Baton Rouge, Louisiana State University Press, 1972.

Kermode, Frank, *Shakespeare, Spenser, Donne*, New York, The Viking Press, 1971.

King, Walter N., ed., *Twentieth Century Interpretations of "Twelfth Night,"* Englewood Cliffs, N.J., Prentice-Hall, 1968.

Knight, G. Wilson, *The Crown of Life: Interpretations of Shakespeare's Final Plays*, London, Oxford University Press, 1947.

Lawrence, William Witherle, *Shakespeare's Problem Comedies*, New York, Frederick Ungar, 1960.

Miles, Rosalind, *The Problem of "Measure for Measure,"* New York, Barnes & Noble Books, 1976.

Muir, Kenneth, ed., *Shakespeare: The Comedies*, Englewood Cliffs, N.J., Prentice-Hall, 1965.

Palmer, David John, ed., *Shakespeare's Later Comedies: An Anthology of Modern Criticism*, Harmondsworth, England, Penguin Books, 1971.

Parrott, Thomas Marc, *Shakespearean Comedy*, New York, Russell & Russell, 1962.

Salingar, Leo, *Shakespeare and the Traditions of Comedy*, London, Cambridge University Press, 1974.

Smith, Hallett, ed., *Twentieth Century Interpretations of "The Tempest,"* Englewood Cliffs, N.J., Prentice-Hall, 1969.

Swinden, Patrick, *An Introduction to Shakespeare's Comedies*, New York, Harper & Row, 1973.

Tillyard, E. M. W., *Shakespeare's Last Plays*, London, Chatto and Windus, 1968.

————, *Shakespeare's Problem Plays*, Toronto, University of Toronto Press, 1950.

Traversi, Derek, *Shakespeare: The Early Comedies*, London, Longmans, Green, 1960.

————, *Shakespeare: The Last Phase*, London, Hollis & Carter, 1954.

Wilson, John Dover, *Shakespeare's Happy Comedies*, Evanston, Ill., Northwestern University Press, 1962.

INDEX

Achilles, 145–46, 149–50
Adam (in *As You Like It*),
    118, 119, 127
Adams, Maude, 127
Adriana, 13, 16, 18–19
Aegeon, 12, 14–15, 62, 94
Aemilia, 12, 15, 21
allegory
    in *Measure for Measure*,
        169–71
    in *Tempest*, 214–16
Allen, Viola, 200
All's Well That Ends Well, 2,
    3, 8, 10, 78, 125, 144, 153–
    160, 161, 162, 187
    plot source, 153–54
    stage history, 159–60
Alonso, 217; 219, 220, 226
American Conservatory
    Theatre, 31, 32–33, 212
Anderson, Mary, 213
Angelo, 161–71, 173, 190
    illustration, 172
Anne Page, 94, 95, 98–100
Antigonus, 202, 204–6, 209
Antiochus, 176–77
Antipholus of Ephesus, 12, 17,
    21
Antipholus of Syracuse, 12–19,
    21
Antonio (in *Merchant of*

Venice), 77, 78, 80–90,
    135, 192
Antonio (in *Tempest*), 216,
    217, 220, 226
Antonio (in *Twelfth Night*),
    131, 134, 135
Antoon, A. J., 114
Apollonius of Tyre, 14, 174
Arden, Forest of, 117, 119–22,
    127, 129, 188
Ariel, 214, 217–22, 224, 225,
    228, 229
    illustration, 227
Armado, 46, 50–53, 58
Armin, Robert, 234n.1
Arviragus, 187–89, 195
As You Like It, 2, 3, 9, 13, 40,
    42, 67, 102, 116–29, 131,
    133, 139, 145, 188, 197, 207,
    222
    illustration, 128
    plot source, 116
    stage history, 127–29
Ashcroft, Peggy, 200
Atkins, Robert, 184
Audrey, 122, 125, 127
Autolycus, 207–8
    illustration, 212

Ball, William, 31, 33
Barber, C. L., 48, 82

Bassanio, 77, 80, 83–85, 89, 105, 135
  illustration, 91
Bawtree, Michael, 59
Beatrice, 11, 50, 103, 105–8, 110–13, 190, 196
Beaumont, Francis, 10, 186
Belarius, 187–89, 193, 195
Benedick, 11, 50, 103, 105–8, 110–14, 123, 135, 190
Benson, Frank R., 74
Berowne, 47–51, 56, 105, 123
  illustration, 59
Berry, Ralph, 72, 101
Bertram, 153–59
Betterton, Thomas, 184
Bianca, 18, 22, 24–28, 30, 83, 105
Blackfriar's Theatre, 3, 186, 216
Boccaccio, Giovanni, 8, 153–155, 187
Bond, Michael, 227
  illustration, 227
Booth, Edwin, 92
Borachio, 104, 108–11
Bottom, 43, 65–67, 69–74, 99, 108, 125
  illustration, 75
boy actress, 122
Boyet, 56–58
Boys from Syracuse, The, 20
Bracegirdle, Anne (Mrs.), 173
Brook, Peter, 74–76, 173, 213
Brooks, Jeff, 141
  illustration, 141
Burbage, Richard, 1, 91
Burton, Richard, 32

Caliban, 214, 217, 220–25, 228–29
  illustration, 227
Campbell, Oscar J., 144
Carver, Brent, 227
  illustration, 227
Celia, 118–19, 122, 123
Chambers, E. K., 143
Chandler, Joan, 229

Charles the wrestler, 117–19
Charlton, H. B., 44, 78, 82, 97, 100–101, 153, 157
Chaucer, Geoffrey, 62, 144
chorus
  in Pericles, 175–76
  in Winter's Tale, 203
Christopher Sly, 23, 32
chronicle tradition, 187
Chronicles (Holinshed), 187
Cibber, Susanna (Mrs.), 173
classicism, 6–7
Claudio (in Measure for Measure), 161–62, 164–71
Claudio (in Much Ado), 102–108, 110–14, 135
Cloten, 189–90, 192–99
clown. See Bottom, Dogberry, Launce. See also fool
Clown (in Winter's Tale), 43, 205, 207–8
  illustration, 212
Comedy of Errors, The, 1, 2, 3, 6–7, 12–21, 22, 26, 42, 62, 94, 131, 134, 135, 174, 182, 216
  illustration, 20
  plot source, 12–13
  stage history, 20–21
commedia dell'arte, 24, 33, 51
Confessio Amantis (Gower), 174
Corin, 120–21, 125, 127
Costard, 43, 45, 50–52, 54, 58, 70, 78, 99, 108
Countess (in All's Well), 154, 156, 158
court comedy, 7–8
Courtezan (in Comedy of Errors), 17–18
courtly love tradition, 8–9, 24–25, 38–40, 42, 49, 105, 116, 123, 131, 132
Covent Garden, 60, 159
Cowl, Jane, 141
Craig, Hardin, 15, 24, 143
Cressida, 144–50, 152
  illustration, 151
Crosman, Henrietta, 127

Cymbeline, 3, 8, 14, 40, 174, 185–200, 201, 203–6, 211, 217, 225
  plot sources, 187
  stage history, 199–200
Cymbeline, King, 187–89, 195, 198, 208

Daly, Augustin, 32, 60, 74, 101, 129
Davenport, Fanny, 127, 200
David, Alan, 128
  illustration, 128
Davis, Daniel, 212
  illustration, 212
Decameron, 8, 153–54, 187
Demetrius, 62–63, 65, 67–68, 72, 83
Diana (in *All's Well*), 155, 157, 159
Diana Enamorada (Montemayor), 34, 67
Dionyza (in *Pericles*), 177, 180
disguise
  in *As You Like It*, 122
  in *Cymbeline*, 197
  in *Measure for Measure*, 168–69
  in *Merchant of Venice*, 86
  in *Twelfth Night*, 133–35
  in *Two Gentlemen of Verona*, 40–41
Doctor Caius, 94, 100
Dogberry, 43, 54, 99, 103, 108–109, 113, 115, 125, 190
Dogget, Thomas, 79, 90
Don John, 103–4, 110–11
Don Pedro, 104, 106–7, 109–112
Drew, John, 32, 60, 101
Dromio of Ephesus, 13, 21, 42
Dromio of Syracuse, 13–14, 19, 21, 42
Drury Lane, 90, 127, 140, 159, 199, 212
Dryden, John, 152, 228
Duke Frederick, 117–18
Duke of Milan, 36, 40, 93

Duke Senior, 117, 119–22, 125, 188
Duke Vincentio, 162–63, 167–71, 173
Dull, 50–51, 53–54, 58
Dumain, 47, 49, 56

Edmondson, Jim, 141
Eglamour, 35
Elizabeth I, 2, 7, 46, 77, 93, 100, 233n.1
Elizabethan Stage Society, 152, 159, 173
Endimion (Lyly), 38
Euphues (Lyly), 7, 51
euphuism, 7–8, 51, 56
Evans, Bertrand, 178, 208, 233n.1
Evans, Edith, 152
Every Man in His Humour (Jonson), 9

fairies
  in *Merry Wives of Windsor*, 95, 97–98, 100
  in *Midsummer Night's Dream*, 63–67, 71, 74–76
Falstaff, Sir John, 7, 93, 95–98, 100–101, 136, 157, 207
farce, 13–15, 28
Fenton, 94, 98, 100
Ferdinand, 217, 222–24, 226, 229
Feste, 42, 125, 131, 139–40, 145, 158, 207
  illustration, 141
First Folio, the, 3, 36, 51, 143, 175
Fletcher, John, 10, 186, 231n.3
Florizel, 205, 207, 223
Fontanne, Lynn, 32
fool. *See* Feste, Lavache, Touchstone, Trinculo. *See also* clown
Forbes-Robertson, Johnston, 91–92, 213
Fortune Theatre, 173
friendship, male
  in *Merchant of Venice*, 83

in *Twelfth Night*, 135
in *Two Gentlemen of
Verona*, 37–40
Fry, Charles, 152

Garrick, David, 32, 74, 113,
199, 211
Gascoigne, George, 22, 24
Gesta Romanorum, 78
Gielgud, John, 213
Gingold, Hermione, 152
Globe Theatre, 2, 3, 127, 205
Gower (in *Pericles*), 174–77,
181–84
Granville-Barker, Harley, 49,
192, 213
Gratiano, 84, 88
illustration, 91
Greene, Robert, 46, 201, 203
Gremio, 24, 27–28
Guiderius, 187–89, 192–93, 195
Guthrie, Tyrone, 45–46, 60,
151, 152, 173
Guthrie Theater, 91

Hall, Elizabeth, 3
Hall, John, 3
Hampden, Walter, 92, 229
Harris, Rosemary, 151
illustration, 151
Harrison, G. B., 24, 46, 153
Hathaway, Anne, 1
Hayes, Helen, 141
Haymarket Theatre, 199
Hector, 146, 149, 150
Helen of Troy, 145–46
Helena (in *All's Well That
Ends Well*), 153–59
Helena (in *Midsummer
Night's Dream*), 62–63,
67–68, 72
Henry IV, 7, 93, 95–96, 98, 157,
207
Henry V, 95–96, 175
Hepburn, Katharine, 127, 141
Hermia, 62–63, 67–68, 72
Hermione, 202–4, 206, 209–
213, 226
Hero, 103–5, 107–13, 190, 209

Hippolyta, 62–63, 72, 93
Hirsch, John, 227
*History of Felix and Philio-
mena, The* (anon.), 34
Holinshed, Raphael, 187
Holofernes, 46, 50–54, 58
Homer, 144, 178
Hopkins, Anthony, 227
illustration, 227
Hortensio, 24, 26–28
Howard, Alan, 75
illustration, 75
Huddleston, Will, 20
Hughes, Barnard, 115
humours comedy, 9–10, 98,
125–26, 136
Huon of Bordeaux, 62

Iachimo, 80, 187, 189, 191–92,
195, 200
Iliad (Homer), 144, 145
imagery, 72–73
Imogen, 11, 40, 187, 189, 191,
193–98, 200, 226
induction, 23–24, 32, 33
Irving, Henry, 79, 90–91, 113,
140, 200
Isabella, 161–66, 168–71,
173, 190
Italianate influence, 8–9, 24
in *Cymbeline*, 187, 195
in *Midsummer Night's
Dream*, 67
in *Much Ado about
Nothing*, 102–4
in *Two Gentlemen of
Verona*, 34

James, Emrys, 128
illustration, 128
Jacquenetta, 50, 54, 58
Jaques, 116, 120–21, 124–27,
129, 207
illustration, 128
Jenkins, Thomas, 46
Jessica, 81, 90
Jew of Malta, The (Mar-
lowe), 77
Johnson, Samuel, 155, 185, 186

Jonson, Ben, 9, 98, 136, 144
Julia, 35, 37, 39–41, 105, 133

Kane, John, 75
    illustration, 75
Katharine (in *Love's Labor's
    Lost*), 49, 55–56
    illustration, 59
Katharine (in *Taming of the
    Shrew*), 18, 22–24, 26–33,
    83
Kean, Charles, 101
Kean, Edmund, 90, 212–13
Kemble, John Philip, 91, 140,
    159, 212
Kempe, Will, 1, 44
Kermode, Frank, 90
Kestelman, Sara, 75
    illustration, 75
King Lear, 80, 178, 179, 187
King of France (in *All's Well
    That Ends Well*), 155,
    156, 158–59
King of Navarre, 47–49, 52, 54,
    56, 60, 93
    illustration, 59
King's Men, 2, 186
Kiss Me, Kate (Porter), 32
Knight's Tale (Chaucer), 62
Kyle, Barry, 172

Lafeu, 154, 156–59
Lamos, Mark, 91
    illustration, 91
Langham, Michael, 91
Langtry, Lily, 127
language, 7–8, 11
    in *Love's Labor's Lost*, 46,
        51–56
    in *Measure for Measure*, 162
    in *Merry Wives of Wind-
        sor*, 93–94
    in *Midsummer Night's
        Dream*, 72–73, 76
    in *Pericles*, 176
    in *Taming of the Shrew*, 32
    in *The Tempest*, 228
    in *Troilus and Cressida*, 145
    in *Twelfth Night*, 132

    in *Two Gentlemen of
        Verona*, 42
    in *Winter's Tale*, 205–6
Laughton, Charles, 173
Launce, 36, 42–44, 70, 78, 108,
    125
Lancelot Gobbo, 78, 80, 108
Lavache, 125, 154, 156, 158
Lawrence, W. W., 155
Lee, Ming Cho, 114, 227
Leonato, 103, 106–7, 109–11
Leontes, 94, 202–4, 206, 208–
    211, 213
Lincoln's Inn Fields, 113
Lodge, Thomas, 116, 124–25
Longaville, 47, 49, 56
Lord Chamberlain's Men, 1, 2,
    234n.1
love quartet
    in *Merchant of Venice*, 83–
        84
    in *Midsummer Night's
        Dream*, 67–69
    in *Much Ado about
        Nothing*, 102
"love-in-idleness," 66–68, 73
Love's Labor's Lost, 1, 2, 7, 8,
    43, 45–60, 61, 63, 69, 70, 78,
    100, 105, 131, 222
    illustration, 59
    stage history, 58–60
Lucentio, 22, 24–27, 105
Luciana, 13, 17, 18
Lucio, 161, 164–65, 169–70,
    180, 190
    illustration, 172
Lunt, Alfred, 32
Lyly, John, 7–8, 37–38, 46, 51
Lysander, 62–63, 65–68, 72, 83

McDowell, Roddy, 229
Macklin, Charles, 90, 140
Macready, William Charles,
    91, 173, 212, 229
Malvolio, 131, 135–38, 140
Maria (in *Love's Labor's
    Lost*), 49, 56
    illustration, 59

Maria (in *Twelfth Night*), 131, 136–39
Mariana (in *Measure for Measure*), 162–63, 165, 168–70
Marina, 179–83
Mark Taper Forum, 221, 227
Marlowe, Christopher, 77, 79
Marlowe, Julia, 32, 113, 141, 200
Marston, John, 144
masque
  in *As You Like It*, 122
  in *Merry Wives of Windsor*, 100
  in *Tempest*, 219, 221–23
Massey, Raymond, 229
Master Ford, 94–97
Mathews, Charles James, 59–60, 74
Measure for Measure, 3, 10, 78, 144, 154, 161–73, 180, 187, 190
  illustration, 172
  plot source, 161
  stage history, 171–73
mechanicals (in *Midsummer Night's Dream*), 69–74
Menaechmi (Plautus), 12–13
Merchant of Venice, The, 2, 40, 77–92, 131, 133, 135, 192
  illustration, 91
  plot sources, 77–78
  Semitic issue in, 77, 79–82
  stage history, 90–92
Meres, Francis, 2
Merry Wives of Windsor, The, 2, 8, 10, 93–101, 121, 136
  operatic version, 101
  plot source, 94
  stage history, 101
Metamorphoses (Ovid), 62
Midsummer Night's Dream, A, 2, 8, 13, 43, 61–76, 100, 116, 121, 217, 222
  illustration, 75
  film version, 74

plot sources, 61–62
stage history, 73–76
miles gloriosus, 7, 157
Miranda, 216–18, 222–24, 228–229
  illustration, 227
mistaken identity, 13–15
Mistress Ford, 94, 96, 101
Mistress Page, 94, 96, 101
Mistress Quickly, 95–96, 98–99, 233n.1
Modjeska, Helen, 200
Montemayor, Jorge de, 34, 67
Moss, Arnold, 229
Moth, 46, 50, 58
Much Ado about Nothing, 2, 10, 43, 50, 54, 67, 102–15, 135, 190, 196, 209
  illustration, 114
  plot source, 103
  stage history, 113–15
multiplotting
  in *Cymbeline*, 185–86, 187
  in *Merchant of Venice*, 77
  in *Merry Wives of Windsor*, 94–95
  in *Midsummer Night's Dream*, 61–63
  in *Much Ado about Nothing*, 102–3

Nahrwold, Thomas M., 212
  illustration, 212
Nathaniel, 46, 50–51, 54, 58
National Theatre (Great Britain), 128–29
Nettles, John, 172
  illustration, 172
New Cambridge text
  of *All's Well That Ends Well*, 153
  of *Measure for Measure*, 163
  of *Merchant of Venice*, 83
  of *Troilus and Cressida*, 144
  of *Twelfth Night*, 130
  of *Two Gentlemen of Verona*, 37
New York Shakespeare Festival, 44, 114, 184

Nunn, Trevor, 128
Nym, 96, 98

Oberon, 62, 63, 65–69, 72, 78, 110, 217
illustration, 75
Old Vic, 45, 92, 151, 152, 173, 184, 200
Oliver, 117–18, 122
Olivia, 131–33, 135–39, 142
Olivier, Laurence, 92
Olster, Fredi, 31, 33
illustration, 31
Oregon Shakespearean Festival, 20, 21, 141, 152
Orlando, 9, 117–19, 121–24, 126
Orsino, 9, 131–35, 139, 142
Othello, 6, 8, 94, 197, 208
Ovid, 62

Palance, Jack, 229
Palladis Tamia (Meres), 2
Pandarus, 144–48, 150
illustration, 151
Pandosto (Greene), 201, 203
Pantalone, 24, 26
Papp, Joseph, 114, 144
Parolles, 154–58
Parrott, Thomas Marc, 215–16
pastoralism
in *As You Like It*, 116, 119–121
in *Cymbeline*, 188
in *Winter's Tale*, 206–7
Patterne of Paynfull Aduentures (Twyne), 174–75
Patroclus, 145–46, 150
Paulina, 202, 204, 206, 208–10, 213
Pecorone, Il, 77
Perdita, 203, 205, 207, 211, 213, 223
Pericles, Prince of Tyre, 3, 14, 174–84, 185, 201, 203, 204, 205, 206, 211, 216, 223, 225
authorship of, 175
plot sources, 174–75
stage history, 183–84
Pericles, 176–84, 223

Petruchio, 11, 22–23, 26–33, 231n.3
illustration, 31
Phelps, Samuel, 20, 32, 60, 74, 91, 173, 184, 212, 229
Philaster (Beaumont and Fletcher), 186
Plautus, 6, 12, 15, 17, 18
play-within-a-play, 23, 46, 63
Plummer, Christopher, 229
Plutarch, 62
Poel, William, 152, 159, 173
Polixenes, 204–5, 223
Portia, 40, 77–78, 83–89, 92, 105, 110, 133
Posthumus Leonatus, 187, 189, 193, 195–99
Princess of France, 47–49, 52–53, 55–56, 60
illustration, 59
Promos and Cassandra (Whetstone), 161
Prospero, 11, 214–20, 222–26, illustration, 227
Proteus, 35–42, 83, 105, 135
Pryce, Jonathan, 172
illustration, 172
Puck, 11, 63–66, 68–69, 72, 217
illustration, 75
"Pyramus and Thisbe," 62, 63, 69, 70, 74

Quayle, Anthony, 200
Queen (in *Cymbeline*), 190–191, 195
Queeny, Thomas, 3
Quiller-Couch, Arthur, 83, 130, 153, 157, 158, 163, 205

raisonneur, 65, 139
realistic comedy, 9–10
Rehan, Ada, 32, 60, 101
Reinhardt, Max, 74
Rich, John, 113
Ridley, M. R., 196
Riehle, Richard, 141
illustration, 141
Robin Goodfellow. *See* Puck
Robson, Flora, 213

Rogers, Paul, 151
  illustration, 151
romance tradition, 8, 174, 183, 186, 189–90, 205, 226–26
Romeo, 35, 146, 147
Romeo and Juliet, 69, 175
Rosalind, 11, 40, 117–19, 121–124, 127, 133–34, 197
Rosaline (in *Love's Labor's Lost*), 48, 49–50, 55–56, 60, 105
  illustration, 59
Rosalynde (Lodge), 116, 124–125
Royal Shakespeare Theatre, 74–75, 129. *See also* Stratford-upon-Avon

Sadler's Wells, 20, 32, 60, 74, 173, 184
Scofield, Paul, 176
Sebastian (in *The Tempest*), 217, 220, 226
Sebastian (in *Twelfth Night*), 131–32, 134–35
Shakespeare, Hamnet (son), 1, 2
Shakespeare, John (father), 2
Shakespeare, Judith (daughter), 1, 3
Shakespeare, Susanna (daughter), 1, 3
Shakespeare, William
  birth of, 1
  death of, 3
  in London, 1–3, 5
  marriage of, 1
  retirement, 3
Shaw, George Bernard, 129, 158, 200
Shepherd (in *Winter's Tale*), 205, 207–8
  illustration, 212
Shylock, 11, 77–82, 84, 86–90, 92
Siddons, Sarah, 173, 212
Silbert, Peter, 141
  illustration, 141

Silvia, 35–39, 41, 43
Sim, Alistair, 200
Simonides, 179, 181, 223
Singer, Marc, 31, 33
  illustration, 31
Sir Andrew Aguecheek, 131, 134, 136–37
  illustration, 141
Sir Hugh Evans, 100
Sir Toby Belch, 131, 136–37
  illustration, 141
Skinner, Otis, 92
Slender, 94, 100, 136
sonnets, Shakespeare's, 38, 51, 52
Sothern, E. H., 32, 113
sources, plot. *See* individual play titles
Speed, 36, 42–43
stage histories. *See* individual play titles
Stephano, 217, 219–21, 225
Stoll, Elmer Edgar, 215
Straight, Beatrice, 141
Stratford (Connecticut), 152, 229
Stratford (Ontario), 59
Stratford-upon-Avon, 1, 2, 3, 46, 74, 159, 172, 173, 176, 184, 215
Supposes (Gascoigne), 22, 24, 25
Swift, Clive, 151
  illustration, 151
Swinburne, A. C., 196

Taming of a Shrew, The (anon.), 22, 23
Taming of the Shrew, The, 1, 3, 18, 22–33, 42, 67, 231n.3
Taylor, Elizabeth, 32
Tempest, The, 3, 10, 125, 143, 159, 174, 203, 214–29
  illustration, 227
  stage history, 228
Terry, Ellen, 113, 200, 213
Thaisa (in *Pericles*), 177, 179, 181–83, 223, 226

Thersites, 145, 150
Theseus, 62–63, 68, 72, 93
Thorndike, Sybil, 200
Tillyard, E. M. W., 158, 206–207
Titania, 63, 65–67, 69, 71–73
    illustration, 75
Touchstone, 42, 116, 119–22, 124–27, 139, 158
    illustration, 128
tragicomedy, 9, 10, 174, 184, 186, 188, 190–94, 201, 202, 204
Tree, Herbert Beerbohm, 92, 213, 229
Trinculo, 125, 217, 219
Troilus, 144–50
Troilus and Crissida, 2, 3, 8, 10, 143–52, 153, 161
    illustration, 151
    plot sources, 144
    stage history, 152
Troilus and Criseyde (Chaucer), 144
Twelfth Night, 2, 3, 9, 10, 13, 14, 40, 42, 67, 102, 125, 130–42, 143, 145, 174, 207
    illustration, 141
    musical adaption, 142
    plot sources, 130–31
    stage history, 140–42
Two Gentlemen of Verona, The, 1, 2, 3, 8, 34–44, 67, 70, 78, 83, 131, 133, 135, 141–42
    musical version, 44
    plot source, 34
    stage history, 44

Twyne, Lawrence, 174
Tynan, Kenneth, 173

Ulysses, 145–46, 149–50
Unities, Three, 216–17

Valentine, 35–40, 42, 83, 135
Vestris, Mme., 60
Viola, 40–41, 131–35, 139–41

Walker, Alice, 144
Walker, Sydney, 212
    illustration, 212
Waller, David, 75
    illustration, 75
Webster, Benjamin, 32
Webster, Margaret, 229
Welsh, Kenneth, 91
    illustration, 91
Whetstone, George, 161
Wilson, John Dover, 46, 60, 79, 99
Winter's Tale, The, 3, 10, 14, 36, 43, 112, 159, 174, 201–213, 216, 223, 225
    illustration, 212
    plot source, 201
    stage history, 211–13
Woffington, Peg, 173
Woman's Prize, The (Fletcher), 231n.3
Wynyard, Diana, 213

Your Own Thing (musical), 142

Zimbalist, Stephanie, 227
    illustration, 227